Acknowledgements

I want to thank my husband, Walter Rappeport, my mother, Mary Wydler; and my friend, Pola Mejía, for all their sustained support throughout this project. I am forever grateful to them. Without their love and encouragement, this book would never have been completed.

Contents

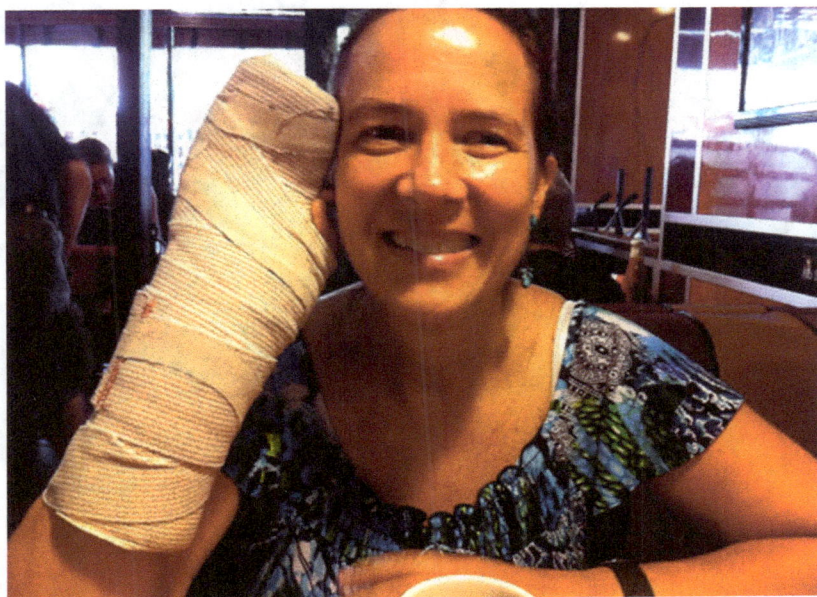

How to Buy Your Home and Not Lose Your Mind!

STEP-BY-STEP GUIDE TO BUYING A HOME IN HOUSTON, TEXAS

Patricia Wydler

Copyright © 2012 Patricia Wydler
All rights reserved.

ISBN: 978-0-9885447-1-0

Typesetting and Layout: www.wordzworth.com

Library of Congress Control #: 2012920815
Homes at Your Fingertips/Home Muscle Series

Appendixes

Disclaimer

This guide is for informational purposes only.

I am not a lawyer, accountant, inspector, insurance agent, or surveyor. I am a real estate broker and hold my loan officer's license to do business in Houston, Texas. Any advice that I give is my opinion, based on my own experience. You should always seek the advice of other relevant professionals before acting on something that I have published or recommended.

This guide includes information about third-party products or services. I do not assume responsibility or liability for any third-party material or opinions.

No part of this publication shall be reproduced, transmitted, or sold, in whole or in part in any form, without the prior written consent of the author. All trademarks and registered trademarks appearing in this guide are the property of their respective owners.

Users of this guide are advised to do their own due diligence when it comes to making home buying decisions and all information, products, services that have been provided should be independently verified by your own qualified professionals.

By reading this guide, you agree that neither my company nor I is responsible for the success or failure of your home buying decisions using any information presented herein.

Introduction

If you have not bought a home, or attempted to buy your first home but did not succeed, you are holding the right book now.

Buying a home is not easy!

It is a complex procedure.

Welcome to the journey!

I am Patricia Wydler, a real estate broker in Houston, Texas since 2005. I have counseled hundreds of buyer clients who have successfully purchased a home, despite their fears and frustrations. This book is intended to serve as a roadmap to guide first-time homebuyers in simple words and plain English.

If you are just at the beginning of the process, I have for you two bits of advice:

1   Take a first-time homebuyer's class and learn all the steps (even if you have a PhD in physics and are very smart), and

2 Hire the right people to represent you: a good loan officer, a good real estate agent, a good home inspector, and a good homeowner's insurance agent.

What do I mean by hiring the right people? I mean that you should hire:

✓ Real professionals who know what they are doing

✓ Real professionals who answer your questions in a prompt and timely fashion (no matter how "dumb" your questions might sound), and

✓ Real professionals who explain to you, in crystal clear language, what is going on behind the scenes.

Interview them face to face (if possible)—not just through Facebook!

Pay close attention to these conspicuous, telling clues that they might give off:

✔ Body language

✔ Thoroughness with which your questions are answered.

For starters, below are a few **no-no's** when interviewing a real estate agent:

✖ The agent is in a rush-rush mode, acting as if you are wasting his or her time.

✖ The agent avoids setting up a face-to-face meeting.

✖ The agent sighs in disgust or rolls eyes when you ask a "dumb" question.

My point here is that you do not want to do business with people who treat you poorly, but rather with people who give you all the attention and respect you deserve.

Wouldn't you want to do business with top-notch professionals who not only offer great customer service, but experienced people who have integrity, honesty, reliability and a strong code of ethics?

If you do not carefully select the professionals who will help you, the home-buying process can become an uncomfortable, nightmarish, confusing experience—a real can of worms.

As the title of this book suggests, you do not want to buy a home only to lose your mind.

I never want you to look like this...

The home-buying process consists of many steps. There are a lot of decisions to be made; a lot of emotions bubbling up to the surface; a lot of skeletons coming out of the closet; a lot of papers that have to be signed that you might not understand; a lot of new terms about which you have no clue; a lot of money you will spend, and a lot of money that you will owe the bank.

No matter how smoothly the home-buying process flows, there are always stumbling blocks along the way. It is easy to get annoyed by little things over which you have no control. Oftentimes, homebuyers get entangled in the blaming "You did it/I did not do it" mode that takes you nowhere.

One homebuyer purchase alone involves the coordinated participation of some twenty professionals (most of them you will never meet since they work behind the scenes). Don't you think that any one of these might make a mistake sometime, somewhere, along the way? Most probably you will agree with me and say, "YES."

And not only that: Imagine that you will be handling an average of thirty to fifty documents containing a lot of legal jargon. Paperwork is a necessary evil while buying a home. Many of these documents you will initial and sign. Are we talking about suffering from information overwhelm?

One of the main hassles many homebuyers experience throughout the process is getting the paperwork completely approved by the lender. Sometimes files get stuck in the pipeline. This can be understandably annoying. Especially when you do not know what is going on behind the scenes and you have no control over decisions that are being made regarding your application. If this happens to you, think of it in a more positive light. Loan processors and underwriters are hired by lenders to protect the bank. Nevertheless, their strict guidelines are also protecting the homebuyer from getting into a bad home-buying situation. Underwriters are your biggest friends in this respect.

Be aware that the correct submission of paperwork is critical in getting a loan, a grant and ultimately closing on your home. Please complete everything that is requested from you promptly and properly.

You will need patience while you buy a home. You have no control over much of what happens behind the scenes. Even if you are a pro-active homebuyer and want to speed up the process, there are times when you will have no choice but to wait for others to do their job on their own schedule.

However, the dynamics that occur during the home-buying process are really fascinating! For one, so many things transpire throughout the process that it becomes a great opportunity to discover things about yourself and others that you would have never expected to discover.

You will realize that the first step I recommend for you to do is to take an eight-hour homebuyer class with a HUD approved agency. This is because I am high on educa-tion and know that the more skills and tools you acquire when buying a home, the better off you will be.

And when you take the class don't be shy of turning on your "asking dumb questions" switch.

Be a pro-active homebuyer. This means pressing the Go button when you get stuck, the Act Now button when you procrastinate, and the Yes button when you get discouraged.

Be more on top of things than any of the people who will be representing you (real estate agent, loan officer, insurance agent and inspector).

Most homebuyers who have successfully bought a home are solvers of problems. Not blamers.

A couple more essential recommendations:

Be aware that during the home-buying process some steps are time sensitive. This means that they need to be completed within a certain time period. Do not take these limits lightly. Sometimes, you will need to hurry and do them as quickly as possible.

This will create some stress and tension that cannot be avoided. For instance: Inspections need to be completed within the option period. If they are not, you might risk your earnest money (if you decide to retract from the contract).

Time sensitive awareness also applies to grants. Grants are free money that federal and local city agencies give away to help first time homebuyers buy a home. Cutoff times or deadlines do exist while applying for grants. If you do not submit the documentation within a certain time period, the opportunity of getting approved for a grant might be lost.

As you read along, you will notice that I have inserted several exclamation points throughout the book. I have intentionally placed them to highlight information that I consider critical and to which you should pay attention.

You are welcome to apply Patricia's "Five C's":

1   Be careful

2   Be clear

3   Be communicative

4   Be creative

5   Be complete

And one more thing:

Run for your life from "joy-killers" whose main job is to make it as hard as possible for you to buy your home.

Seek out professionals who are seasoned, have seen it all, and who retain their sense of delight in using their skills to help you.

The purpose of this guide is to make buying your home as interesting and pleasurable as possible.

How to read this book

The sequence of the chapters is based on the sequence of the steps that you need to follow to buy a home. In this sense, the book serves as a guide and point of reference.

The appendixes and the glossary that you find at the end of the book, will also be helpful while reading the book and while undergoing the process of purchasing your home. They are made up of lists, diagrams, definitions, and tables that respond quickly to your questions, and serve as a "checklist" while gathering your documents.

Now, if You Do Not Mind, a Little About Me

I started working in real estate eight years ago. Eight rewarding years of helping clients every day, seeing their dreams of homeownership come true!

My passion is helping first-time homebuyers access the down payment assistance programs available to those who qualify.

Who wouldn't want to receive $30,000 of grant money to buy a home?

In my career, I had the priceless opportunity to build a homeownership center from scratch for Avenue CDC, a nonprofit organization in Houston, Texas. This association provides homeownership workshops for first time buyers with the intention of teaching clients how to make a sound home-buying purchase that is within their budget.

During that time, I counseled many clients who eagerly wanted to buy their first home but did not know how. Most of them experienced confusion and difficulty in understanding how the process worked.

Soon I discovered that people who educated themselves about how to buy a home were less stressed out, felt more empowered, and were far happier than those who did not prepare themselves.

Although the home-buying process is complex, it can also be an exciting, educational experience—and a thought-provoking eye-opener!

Yes, it is true that there are a lot of steps involved, and the process can be scary. But if you learn the steps, you will be more secure, and it will be that much easier.

I encourage you to follow all the steps outlined throughout the book. It will not only help you avoid a lot of common first-time homebuyer mistakes, but will help you make the process, more understandable and pleasurable.

Though I have put forth a huge amount of time and effort trying to explain the process in the simplest possible way, many concepts will still sound foreign to you. Don't expect to learn everything in one sitting. Just take your time, and take one step at a time. If you run across a term you do not understand, or a question pops up in your head that you want answered, do not hesitate to ask the professionals who are representing you.

Finally, I'll leave you with a positive note: Here's an uplifting musical homebuyer video specially prepared for you to jumpstart your home-buying process:

http://animoto.com/play/CmUs0FLEBbS0A8j9p6f10w

A Little About Syed

Five years ago, I met Syed in a furniture store. We got talking about buying a home. His eyes sparkled with enthusiasm when he told me how much he wanted to buy a home, but how difficult he thought it would be.

Three years later, I visited Syed at the store again. He was still fearful, but this time his excitement and courage were greater. He decided to take the leap.

Syed took a little while to become a homebuyer simply because he shared the reservation and anxieties many first time homebuyers have when they start the process.

Throughout the home-buying process Syed made excellent choices. For one, he was never interested in buying a flashy home to impress others. He had the good sense to look for a home within his budget, where his monthly housing payments never went beyond a certain limit that he had set upon himself.

Syed refused to be house poor.

Syed closed on his home in February 2012. He had the good fortune of receiving grant money to purchase his home. This has allowed him to keep his monthly housing expenses low and affordable.

Step 1

Taking an Eight-Hour Home-Buying Class

I cannot stress strongly enough the importance of becoming an educated homebuyer before you buy a home.

You will learn boatloads!

Below is an example/syllabus of Avenue CDC, which is one, of several HUD housing approved non-profit organizations that offer an eight-hour homeownership class:

1   Introduction to Homeownership: The advantages and responsibilities of buying your own home.

2   All About Mortgages: Qualifying for a loan, credit issues, interest rates, types of loans (fixed vs. adjustable, conventional vs. FHA or VA loans), fees and points, pre-payment penalties, good faith estimates and more.

3   Subsidies: Grants and special loans available to low and moderate-income homebuyers.

4   Finding Your Dream Home: Role of realtors, what to look for when shopping for a home.

5   The Pre-Purchase Process: About the earnest money contract, inspections, surveys, appraisals, title insurance.

6   The Closing: Documents and funding

7   After you Have Purchased Your Home: Insurance issues, property taxes, lender communications, homestead exemption, maintenance of a home, avoiding foreclosure.

Below is a link containing a list of HUD approved organizations that offer the eight-homebuyer class in Houston, Texas. Taking this class is a mandatory requirement for all those wanting to get grants and who are eligible to get them: http://www.houstontx.gov/housing/homebuyer.html

BIG TIP: Even if you do not qualify for grants, I highly recommend you take this class.

For one, taking a homeownership class is a great opportunity to get an overall view of the home buying process from beginning to end. In addition, it allows face-to-face interaction with instructors and other homebuyers to get questions answered and clarify confusing concepts.

Most homebuyers who have taken the class have been pleasantly surprised to find out that these classes offer invaluable information in many topics about which they did not know anything.

Furthermore, the material taught, has equipped them with priceless tools and skills that have allowed them to make sounder, smarter and more solid home purchases.

The great advantage of these classes is that most of them are set up as workshops. This allows for hands on training where students are encouraged to participate by doing different kinds of exercises.

Most of these are very beneficial like calculating for how much loan you qualify, and how much home you can afford in monthly housing expenses.

You will be able to benefit from the wealth of information that practicing real estate professionals and instructors have regarding the most common mistakes homebuyers make while buying a home, and how to avoid them.

While taking the class remember:

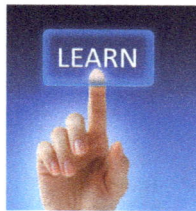

Step 2

Meeting with a Homebuyer Counselor

Homebuyer counselors work for non-profit housing organizations. Their job is to provide you with an objective, overall picture of the home buying process.

The best time to meet with a homebuyer counselor is after you have taken the eight-hour class.

There are many advantages of meeting with a homebuyer counselor:

They understand how realtor and loan officers work. They focus their attention on preparing the homebuyer to become a smarter and pro-active consumer.

If the client is facing credit challenges, the homebuyer counselor supports the client in rebuilding his credit and improving his finances.

Below is a list of services provided by most homebuyer counselors:

- Pulls credit. Teaches homebuyer how to read and evaluate a credit report, and determine a plan of action to rebuild their credit (if it merits rebuilding).

- Assists homebuyer in making a budget: analysis of expenses, income and savings.

- Establishes goals and specific actions to improve spending habits and management skills to rebuild financial habits.

- Qualifies you to see if you are eligible to be approved for a loan. Provides worksheets that teach you how to prequalify yourself from the point of view of the bank.

- Provides you with a wealth of information about grants or down payment assistance programs.

- Clarifies your home buying questions, and offers multiple resources and tools that will be useful throughout the home buying process. These resources, like independent development accounts, and credit re-building organizations, offer useful educational opportunities, free of charge to help you rebuild your credit and save money for pre-closing costs before buying a home.

You may go to: www.houstonhousing.org to find a list of agencies in Houston that provide homebuyer-counseling services.

Step 3

Understanding Credit

If you have not done so already with the homebuyer counselor, or with a bank, the third step I recommend in home buying is to pull your credit. It is a good idea to pull your own credit report before the lender does, so that if there is any incorrect information you can correct it before the lender sees any error. Most credit reports contain mistakes and can reflect wrong information.

When you pull your credit YOURSELF, your scores do not go down at all (this is called a soft hit, soft inquiry, or soft pull). However, when somebody else pulls your credit, your scores will go down by a few points. This is called a hard hit, hard inquiry, or hard pull. If you decide to loan shop to compare prices, and allow many lenders to pull your credit at one given time (about one month), all these pulls should not bring your credit scores down more than the "cost of a single pull." But if you dance around and let several creditors pull your credit over an extended period of time, you will take one or more hard hits and your scores will go down. So be organized.

You will soon discover what a powerful piece of information a credit report is. For one, it is a reflection of your payment habits and spending patterns. It shows how much money you owe, how frequently you use your credit and if you pay your bills on time.

Though there are many sources through which you can pull your credit, I recommend: www.annualcreditreport.com. The reason I prefer this site, to others, is that Annual Credit Report is the only authorized source for the free annual credit report that's yours by law. The purpose of this site is that it offers the consumer the legal right to get one free report a year and dispute mistakes that erroneously appear in that credit report.

Whichever service you choose for pulling your credit, always be aware of their terms of service. Some agencies try to sell you a monthly credit monitoring membership, which you might not want.

You will notice that the home page at www.annualcredit-report.com has the names of three companies: **Experian**, **Transunion**, and **Equifax**. They are credit bureaus, the largest compilers of financial information about consumers in the United States. If you are serious about buying a home, you should pull your credit from each one of them. But wait until you are ready to act.

Although the information about your credit that each one of these agencies has is similar, it is never exactly the same. Some of them have some information that the others do not. Scores also vary slightly from bureau to bureau, because each one uses its own formula to calculate. Most banks rely on these three companies to get a more thorough opinion about your finances.

If you feel that pulling your own credit is overwhelming, you can certainly ask a homebuyer counseling agency or a bank to do it for you (they often charge a fee).

You will have the opportunity to sit down with a home-buyer counselor or a loan officer to evaluate your credit report and what you need to do to improve it, if necessary, to get approved for a loan.

Just be aware that if the bank pulls your credit, your scores might go down a little and you might not be given a hard physical copy of your report. You can request hard copies from each of the credit bureaus.

What will your credit report reveal?

Fasten your seat belts!

They tell so much about you that it might surprise you!

- Each of the three major credit bureaus (Experian, Transunion, and Equifax) has a score for you.

- Reports show your payment history for the last five to seven years.

- They show you whether you paid on time or not—if you were ever 30, 60, 90, or 120 days late—or if you stopped paying a creditor altogether.

- They show any past delinquencies.

- They show how much you owe your creditors (total and monthly balances).

- They show how much you have used of the credit provided to you. For example, it would show that you charged $500 on a credit card with a $1,000 limit.

- They show any collection companies who may have tried to collect debts from you (and whether they were medical debts), as well as whether the debts were sold to other companies.

- They show whether you have disputed any collections, and if so, what were the results.

- They show whether any judgments have been filed against you.

- They show any unpaid taxes owed to the Internal Revenue Service.

- They show apartment evictions and any related legal judgments.

- They show any outstanding student loans.

- They show voluntary or forced car repossessions.

- They can show little things that you would never have imagined, like library late fees.

- They show home foreclosures (when the bank takes a house back for mortgage nonpayment).

- They show the date of real estate short sales (selling a home for less than what is owed to the bank) and the results of the transaction.

- They show bankruptcies.

- They show a list of your past employers.

- They show all your addresses where you've lived in the past seven years.

And more...

In other words, a lot of personal information is gathered in your credit report. If you claim that any of it is not true, you will have to prove it.

Credit reports are known to contain mistakes. You have the legal right to dispute any mistakes—and you should.

Banks use credit reports to decide whether or not to lend you money. It gives them a quick, efficient snapshot of your past financial history and your projected future payment history.

And whether we like it or not, **banks call the shots!**

Pulling your credit might actually be a positive surprise. Many people who think their credit is bad discover that it isn't.

The following chart shows how creditors see the range of scores.

Traditional Credit Scoring

A	680 and over	Good!
A-	620–680	Okay, you can get a loan!
B	580–620	Not very good!
C	500–580	No good!
D-F	Below 500	I have nothing to say! Except, this can be rebuilt!

Nowadays, even though you have a very good chance of getting preapproved with a 640 score, I recommend you **aim for higher.**

Why?

1   The higher your credit score, the easier it will be for you to get a better loan with a better interest rate.

2   The stronger you feel financially, the more empowered you will feel as a homebuyer.

And an empowered homebuyer is what I want you to be: A homebuyer with muscle!

The pie chart below will show you how credit bureaus determine your scores.

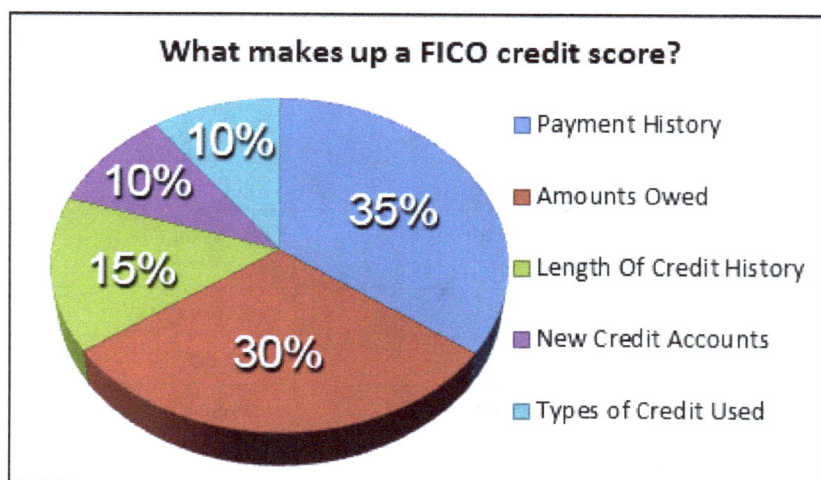

What makes up a FICO credit score?

- Payment History — 35%
- Amounts Owed — 30%
- Length Of Credit History — 15%
- New Credit Accounts — 10%
- Types of Credit Used — 10%

This means:

Thirty percent of your credit score depends on the amount of debt you have.

If you have lots and lots of debt, your credit scores will go down. When banks issue a credit card, they set a maximum limit on what you can borrow. Some of us can get crazy and use almost all the credit we have available. For example, if you charge $900 on a $1000 limit card, you have used almost all of its available credit. You would be what we call "maxed out." Not good!

Credit counselors suggest that consumers use, at most, 40 percent of the allowed limit. For example, if your limit is $1,000, don't charge more than $400. The closer you get to maxed out, the worse off you will be and the lower your credit scores will be.

When banks pull your credit they will be able to quickly spot the amount of debts you have and compare it to your total monthly gross income. The higher monthly debt you have, the less money they will lend you. The reason for this is that lenders want to make sure you can afford to pay them back before they provide you with a loan.

One way they figure your ability to repay is by making sure that your total debt does not exceed certain percentage of your income, usually 36-42%. This percentage is called the debt to income ratio.

To understand this even further let's look at the following fictional example:

- John Smith goes to a bank to get pre-approved for a loan.

- The loan officer checks John's gross income, which is $3,000 per month.

- He also checks his total monthly debts and notices that John has $1,500 of credit card bills to pay each month. Look at the pie below:

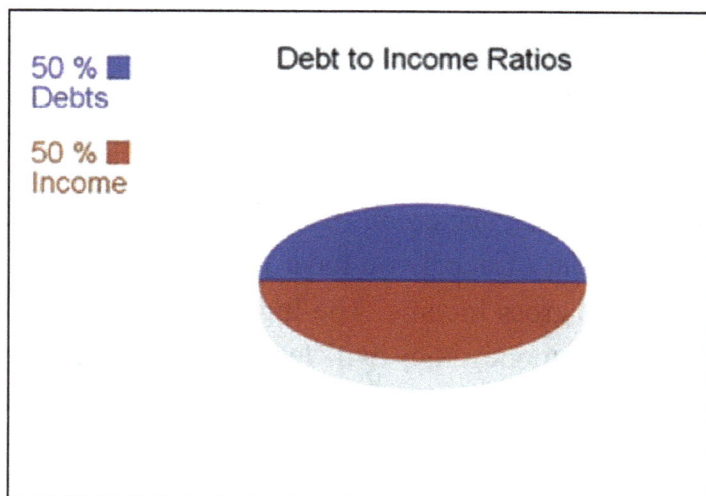

- Half of John's income (the red portion) is used to pay outstanding debt. John has only half left over to pay for anything else. Not good! The banks see John as a great risk to them. They envision him struggling not only to pay the mortgage, but the other $1,500 credit card debt he has as well.

- After seeing this, the loan officer recommends to John to lower his monthly debts and come back at a future date. Otherwise, based on his large monthly debt, the bank could only lend him $26,000. This is certainly not enough to buy a home in Houston.

- John decides to buckle down, pays off all his debt in a year, and reapplies for a mortgage. Now the loan officer pre-qualifies him for $126,000.

Thirty-five percent of your credit score depends on your past payment history. If you have paid anything 30, 60, 90, or 120 days late in the recent past or stopped paying anything altogether, your scores will go down considerably.

Banks pay more attention to recent payment history than to old payment history.

The key point to remember is that you should always pay on time. If you aren't good at managing payment schedules, set up an automated payment system through your bank that withdraws money from your account automatically.

Try to pay more than the minimum due. This will allow you to get rid of your debt as quickly as possible.

Let me show you a **telling example**:

Let's say you buy a $10.00 pizza with a credit card and make only the minimum payment. Over an eighteen-month period, at an 18 percent interest rate, the pizza would end up costing you $42.40!

Fifteen percent of your credit score depends on how long your credit history is.

If you have never applied for a credit card before, you may actually have no credit score at all. Conversely, ten years of positive credit history gets a good score. Banks like to see long credit histories, especially if they are good!

! If you have no credit history whatsoever, I recommend that you start establishing credit by applying for a credit card. Please…**pay on time!** It can take from three to six months before you see any kind of activity on your credit report.

Ten percent of your credit score depends on what new credit you have applied for.

! Don't apply for a lot of new credit cards before (or while) you buy a home! It can really turn against you. Nowadays, banks tend to pull your credit twice—once at the beginning of the process, and once at the very end. If the bank finds out that you have incurred more credit card debt, your loan might be turned down, and you will not be able to buy your home. If you decide to apply for a car loan to buy a car, while you are searching for a home, this will affect your debt ratios considerably, and lenders will not be able to approve you for the initial amount for which they had decided to approve you.

Remember, every time somebody other than you pulls your credit, it lowers your scores! Guess what will happen if you open credit cards from five different department stores while buying a home? More important, the bank will notice that you have incurred new credit. Their train of thought will be: Why is this person getting all these credit cards just before buying a home? It sends the wrong message to the bank. They will consider you a greater risk to them. Not good! The point here is that the bank does not want homebuyers to owe money that could interfere with them paying their mortgage.

! Stay on the conservative side. Though there is no real magic number of credit cards you should have, two is probably enough.

! Apply for cards with the lowest interest rates. Department store cards charge higher rates than bank-based cards like those in the Visa or MasterCard networks.

Ten percent of your credit score depends on the right mix of debt types.

Banks like to see both revolving credit cards (where you have the option of paying only the minimum each month), and fixed installment loans (such as car payments or student loans) on a report.

Pulling your credit can be a rewarding experience if it turns out yours is good. It can be exciting, educational, exhilarating, and ego boosting! Good credit reflects positively on your character.

However, seeing a report that shows you don't have good credit can be a shock, so be prepared!

If this is you, please do not get discouraged! Bad credit does not last forever! It is not permanent. You can do something about it. You can change it. Mind you, it will not be overnight. It will not be a quick fix. It will take time, money, and energy. Sound and sustainable improvements on credit happen only when a person takes full responsibility of their financial life and unhealthy spending patterns are removed and replaced by healthy financial habits.

Whether you have good, bad, or so-so credit, I suggest you do something about it.

If your credit is *bad*, take action and rebuild it! Local nonprofit organizations offer free credit rebuilding classes. Here in Houston, I recommend:

www.creditcoalition.org
www.wesleyhousehouston.org

If your credit is *good*, what are you waiting for?

Get approved for a loan!

Step 4

Making a Budget:
Income, Expenses, and Savings

Before I delve into the budget chapter, let me show you some revealing clipart items I found on the Internet that apply to budgeting.

In the first image, we see a belt tightening around a dollar, almost as if to strangle it to death. Ouch, that hurts! Next, we see sharp scissors cutting a debt sign. Again: ouch!

All this implies that making a budget is hard work. Many people associate making a budget with punishment. No wonder lots of us don't like them! They can seem scary and painful.

I encourage you to get out of punishment mode and into praiseworthy mode while making your budget.

You will soon discover, that no matter how unpleasant making a budget may seem to you, it is one of the best exercises any homebuyer should do before buying a home.

When you make a budget of your expenses, savings and income you will discover worthwhile information about your financial patterns. For one, you will learn where your hard earned income goes. Many times, unsuspectingly so, it is spent on small, "innocent buys" or "trivial expenses"

www.homesatyourfingertips.com

that can amount to a lot of money. Some of these could be called money-wasters, that if applied to something different, could have a productive and promising use.

To make a budget, gather three kinds of information:

1   Your total household income

2   Your total savings

3   A list of all your expenses (daily, monthly, quarterly, and annual)

Feel free to use the following worksheets:

Total Household Income Worksheet

Figure Your Monthly Income

(Choose one of three following methods to calculate your income)

Your weekly take-home pay	$_____	x 52 ÷ 12 =	$_____
Your twice a month take-home pay	$_____	x 2 =	$_____
Your monthly take-home pay	$_____		$_____

Figure Your Spouse's Monthly Income

Your spouse's weekly take-home pay, or	$_____	x 52 ÷ 12 =	$_____
Your spouse's twice a month take-home pay, or	$_____	x 2 =	$_____
Your spouse's monthly take home pay	$_____		$_____

Other Monthly Income

Second job	$
Regular overtime	$
Public assistance	$
Child support	$
Pension	$
Social security	$
Other	$
Other	$

Total Net Monthly Income: $_____

Total Net Annual Income: $_____

Housing Affordability Worksheet

Multiply your gross annual income by 2.5 $_____ x 2.5 =_____ Gross Annual Income Example: $40,000 x 2.5 = $100,000	Low range of housing cost (this means you are using a comfortable and reasonable amount of your income to pay for housing costs).
Multiply your gross annual income by 3.5 $_____x 3.5 =_____ Gross Annual Income Example: $40,000 x 3.5 = $ = $140,000	High range of housing cost (this means you are using a great amount of your income to pay for housing costs).

Total Savings Worksheet

Regular savings account	$
Certificates of deposit	$
Money market accounts	$
Matched savings accounts	$
401K investment account	$
Roth IRA Account	$
Other	$
Other	$
Other	$
Other	$

List of Monthly Expenses Worksheet

Housing

Rent or mortgage	$
Heating (gas or oil)	$
Electricity	$
Cable	$
Water or sewage	$
Telephones (landlines and cell phones)	$
Internet service	$
Trash service	$
Home maintenance expenses	$
Other housing expenses	$
Other housing expenses	$

Transportation

Gas	$
Car payment	$
Car insurance	$
Car inspection	$
Car repairs and maintenance	$
License plates and registration fees	$
Public transportation or taxi	$
Parking and tolls	$

Food

Groceries	$
School lunches	$

Medical

Medical insurance	$
Doctor	$
Dentist	$
Prescriptions	$

Clothing

Clothing	$
Laundry and dry cleaning	$

Debts

Student loan	$
Credit card monthly minimum	$
Credit card monthly minimum	$
Credit card monthly minimum	$
Credit card monthly minimum	$
Credit card monthly minimum	$
Car loan monthly installment	$
Personal loan monthly installment	$

Education

Tuition	$
Books, papers and supplies	$
Newspapers and magazines	$
Lessons (sports, dance, music)	$
Computer related expenses	$

Entertainment

Movies, sporting events, concerts etc.	$
Video rental	$
Restaurants	$
Vacation trips	$
Other	$
Other	$
Other	$
Other	$

Others

Others	$
Others	$
Others	$
Others	$
Others	$
Others	$

Once you complete these exercises, you will have a stronger handle on your expenses, so you can find better ways to cut costs and have more disposable income.

If you have no savings, some nonprofit organizations offer **Independent Development Accounts.**

They work like this:

- You open a savings account with an IDA program.

- You are required to deposit a minimum each month.

- The IDA will match your savings by a factor of two or three.

For example, John saves $1,000 over six months. At the end of that period, the IDA matches his $1,000 with $2000. John now has $3,000 to apply toward closing costs or his down payment.

Note that IDA programs have specific income guidelines, and that you need to be in the program for at least six months. A good resource for IDA services in Houston is www.covenantcapital.org.

Before closing this chapter, I'll leave you with one more thing to think about. Answer my next question as honestly as you possibly can. It will be probably the most important question I shall ask you in this whole book.

How much money would you feel **COMFORTABLE** paying per month in housing expenses after you close on your home?

The key word here is COMFORTABLE.

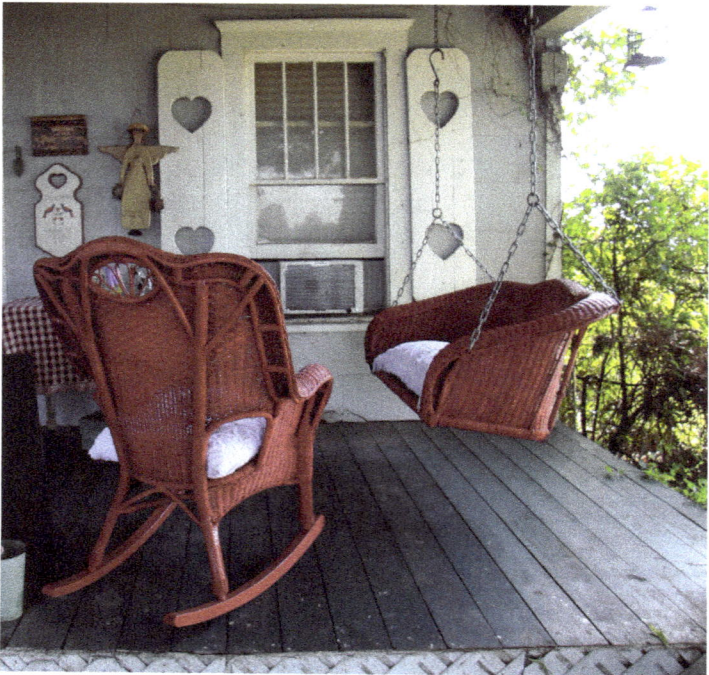

Think for a moment:

Your bank might approve you for a larger loan than you want. I really don't want you to be house poor. *House poor* means that too much of your income goes toward paying for the house, leaving you struggling for money each and every month to pay your other expenses.

Not a good idea!

Don't be house poor!

Do not accept more loan money than you know you can repay comfortably, no matter how flattering it is to be approved for so much.

Always have disposable income available to you and your family.

Always ask:

Step 5

Think Like a Bank: The Five C's

Banks use the Five C's to decide whether or not to approve you for a loan:

Credit

One of the best ways for a lender to tell if you will repay your home loan is to check how you have managed other debts. This is why one of the first steps a bank will take when you apply for a loan is to pull your credit. The credit report will show the bank if you have paid the money you have borrowed on time, the amounts of debts you have incurred over time, and overall your spending patterns and the financial handling of your money.

Capacity

Capacity refers to your ability to earn enough income to make the new mortgage loan payments and still pay all of your other living expenses. Banks prefer borrowers who show they have had a steady stream of income for the past two years. They will look at your current income to see that you earn enough to pay the new house payment and still be able to pay your other expenses.

Capital

The amount of cash or liquid assets, such as savings, pension plans, investments is your capital. The more cash you have in savings accounts, certificates of deposit, bonds, and so on, the more confident the lender will be to lend you money.

Condition

Banks want to know what your present condition is. A loan application asks for a lot of personal information: your employment history, your rental history, your legal status, whether you are married or single, whether you have children and how many, whether you have bank accounts and what type, and so on.

Collateral

Banks want to know if you have other assets that could be used as an alternate repayment source for the loan. Your new home will become collateral, or extra security for your loan. Your lender will investigate all the condition of the house you want to buy to make sure it is worth at least as much money as you are borrowing. Other items that are also used as collateral are a car, furniture, jewelry, or another piece of real estate.

Step 6

Think Like Patricia: The Five C's

SLOW DOWN

Be Careful

As I have mentioned earlier, buying a home is a complex procedure. There are so many steps, so many decisions to be made, so many people involved in the transaction, that it is easy to forget small things that can become big problems. For instance, attention to detail and alertness to specifics are critical towards having a successful home-purchase. I encourage you to stop the "rush-rush/multitasking" mode that leads to sloppy thinking, and sloppy doing. Turn on the "slow down/one step at a time" switch (except for deadline paperwork).

Be Clear

Buying a home can be a puzzle. Un-puzzle yourself! Understand the loan and home terminology. Get somebody who is knowledgeable to explain to you concepts that are difficult to grasp. Break things into little pieces. Do the exercises offered in the homebuyer workshops. Do your own home affordability calculations. Meet face to face with a homebuyer counselor to discuss fears you might have and dispel mis-conceptions you might harbor. Rid yourself from old cobwebs created by confusion and complexity.

Be Communicative

Be a pro-active homebuyer. Keep in touch with the professionals that represent you. Collaborate with your lender and real estate agent when more information is requested. Practice courtesy, respect for others, and good manners with those working on your behalf. Submit paperwork promptly and properly. Make the phone calls you need to make. Don't wait for others to call you.

Be Creative

Tap into your ability of being resourceful. Whenever you run across a snag or hit a bump, think of alternative ways to solve a problem. Brainstorm ideas with your loved ones. Find solutions to problems. Search different ways of getting results. Be open- minded and listen to new suggestions. Buying a home can be a fun experience!

Be Complete

Dig deep. Be thorough! Inspect what is underneath the surface. Investigate what is behind the walls. Envision what is beyond words. Be on top of things. Follow up frequently. Double check with the professionals you hired to make sure they are doing what they are supposed to do. Don't take for granted that somebody else is going to do something they need to do. Sometimes they don't. Often times a file gets stuck in the pipeline for small details that were not taken care of properly. Read documents carefully. Verify information that needs corroboration. If you are doubtful about what decisions to make, create a spreadsheet and compare options. Be detail oriented and understand what you are signing.

Step 7

Meeting with a Loan Officer

You'll work with a loan officer at the bank or mortgage company to get your home loan.

Your loan officer will request from you information provided in the following checklist:

Loan Documentation Checklist

- ☐ Income tax returns of the last two years
- ☐ W-2's or 1099 of the last two years
- ☐ Last two months of paystubs from your employer
- ☐ Bank statements (checking and savings) of the last two months
- ☐ Copy of your driver's license and your social security
- ☐ Statement of stocks, bonds, 401K's, Roth IRA's
- ☐ Letters from landlords stating where you have lived for the past two years
- ☐ Evidence of child support payment (if it applies to you)
- ☐ Evidence of pension payments (if it applies to you)
- ☐ Social security benefits (if it applies to you)
- ☐ Letters of explanation for any negative credit item (if it applies to you)
- ☐ Certified copies of divorce decree (if it applies to you)
- ☐ Veteran's certificate of eligibility (if it applies to you)

When you go in for your consultation, also bring your credit report, if you've pulled one, and ask for an opinion.

If things don't look good, you can avoid having the bank pull your credit at this time. But if you are told you have a good chance of getting preapproved, you can have the bank pull it if you feel comfortable going forward with the loan process.

When you meet with your loan officer, be sure to get a clear explanation of all of the following terms and conditions:

What type of loan you are getting?

There are several kinds:

1   **Conventional loans.** Provided by private institutions. Usually these loans require from the buyer higher credit scores, lower debt to income ratios, mortgage insurance, and usually a higher down payment (but not necessarily). Debt to income ratios is 28/36 percent. The advantage of conventional loans is that their mortgage insurance premiums are usually much lower than FHA loans.

2   **FHA or Federal Housing Administration loans** are also offered by private lenders, but insured by the American government. The rates and fees are set by the government, and not by individual lenders who make the loans. Rules about lending decisions are also established by the government. The interest rate is usually

lower, or the same as rates from conventional loans. The debt to income ratios is generally 29/41. With FHA loans, down payment is normally 3% and you are required to pay a monthly mortgage insurance premium until the outstanding principal balance of your loan reaches 78% loan to value. Mortgage insurance premium is mandatory for a period of five years, whether or not you have reached the 78% loan to value mark.

FHA limits the maximum money you can borrow. This could be a good option for credit challenged borrowers since requirements are not so strict as conventional lenders. The downside of FHA loans is that mortgage insurance is higher than conventional loans. It also charges an extra upfront insurance premium that conventional loans do not charge. This extra amount increases closing costs.

3 **Veteran Association Loans** are only offered to veterans or to direct relatives of veterans. The veteran does not have to provide a down payment. The veteran does have to pay some closing costs and a 1% funding fee. The debt to income ratios is usually both 41%.

4 **Fixed Rate Mortgages.** Mortgages where interest remains the same for the life of the loan. Keep in mind that property taxes and insurance fees, that are also part of your monthly housing expenses, are not fixed.

They do vary from year to year. A fixed rate loan is the most common type of loan and the best for a first time homebuyer.

5 **Adjustable Rate Mortgages** or ARMS usually start out at an interest rate below the average fixed rate. However after a certain amount of years they adjust (increase or decrease). ARMS have caps on the amount of interest that can be charged. An ARM may allow you to buy a more expensive home because the introductory interest rate is low. However, you might get into trouble when the rates begin to adjust and your payments become higher than you realized.

Monthly housing expenses

You want to be crystal clear about what you will have to pay the bank every month after you buy the home. For example, John and Mary are buying a $150,000 home. Their numbers look like this:

Sales price	$150,000
Loan amount	$120,000
Down payment	$30,000
Interest rate	5.625
Estimated property taxes	3%
Homeowners' Association fees	None

The loan officer does some calculations and shows the buyers a **breakdown** of their monthly housing expenses based on a $120,000 loan:

Principal and Interest	$693.09
Property taxes	$376.25
Homeowner's insurance	$70.23
Homeowners' Association fees	$0.00
Total monthly housing expenses	$1,139.57

In other words, John and Mary will have to pay an estimated **$1,139.57** per month in housing expenses.

There is a quick and useful **rule of thumb** that homebuyers can apply when calculating average monthly housing expenses. It is called **the 1% average.**

What this means is that you will have to pay aroundt 1% of a home's sales price a month for housing expenses (these include principal, interest, property taxes, homeowner's insurance, and private mortgage insurance).

For example, let's say you fall in love with a magnificent Victorian-style home priced at $300,000. Using the 1% average, you would know immediately that it would cost about $3,000 every month. These $3,000 include only housing expenses (principal, interest, property taxes, homeowner's insurance and private mortgage insurance). Utility expenses such as water, electricity, and gas are not included. And of course food is not included either.

Can you afford it? Remember that the 1% average is only an **estimate,** not an **exact** figure.

Interest rate

Interest rates make a big difference in your monthly housing payments and your closing costs. This is a critical topic that you should discuss with your loan officer.

See chart below:

Loan amount	Interest	Principal and Interest	Total Cost in interest charges	Loan term
$50,000	10%	$439.00	$108,040	30 years
$50,000	7%	$333.00	$69,880	30 years

Let me alert you that when you get a fixed interest loan, the only parts of your monthly payment that will stay fixed over the term of the loan are the principal and interest amounts. Property tax and homeowner's insurance (that are also part of your monthly housing expenses) will most probably increase over the years.

Since the beginning of your home search ask yourself what is the percentage of property tax rate you will have to pay. Neighborhoods that are located in excellent school districts tend to charge a higher property tax rate.

Closing Costs

By law, a lender must give you a document called a *Good Faith Estimate*. It contains a breakdown of closing expenses. Ask your loan officer if any of the closing costs are negotiable. **Closing costs can range from 3 to 7 percent of the loan amount.**

Pre-Closing Costs

These are items you pay for before you actually sign a mortgage. They usually include:

- Credit report (paid to the lender)
- Earnest money (paid to the title company)
- Appraisal report (paid to the lender)
- Home inspection (paid to the inspector)

I always tell buyers to have at least $2,000 of available cash to pay for these pre-closing costs.

Down Payment

It is the amount of cash you pay towards the sales price. It varies from loan to loan. FHA loans for example, require homebuyers to bring approximately 3 percent of the sales price. Conventional loans might ask for more, 5 percent. Some loans will accept zero down payments.

Truth in Lending

The lender must also give you this document shortly after you sign a loan application. It has four boxes containing important information about the costs of the loan. Following you can see an example of a Truth in Lending diagram for a loan in the amount of $120,400.

Annual Percentage Rate	Finance Charge	Amount Financed	Total amount of payments
The cost of your credit as a yearly rate 5.9505%	The dollar amount the credit will cost you. $133,295.21	The amount of credit provided to you on your behalf $116,217.67	The amount you will have paid after you have made all payments as scheduled $249,512.88

1 Annual Percentage Rate:

The first thing to understand is that Annual Percentage Rate is different from your regular interest rate.

It is always more, because it includes closing fees and upfront fees calculated as a percentage of the loan amount.

! APR is an important indicator to watch for when you are shopping for a loan. A higher APR indicates that there will be more closing costs. It goes away when your loan is closed because it indicates how much money, if any, will be required at closing.

Note that the APR on your mortgage is not the same as the APR on your credit card account.

For example, let's say Mary and John go shopping for a loan. They visit the following banks and mortgage companies and are quoted completely different APRs:

Lender	Interest	APR
Bank ABC	6.625%	6.95%
Industry Bank	6.625%	7%
Mortgage XYZ	6.625%	7.5%

Mary and John notice that the banks provide them with the exact same interest rate, but the APRs vary, since they include the closing costs the bank will charge at the closing table. They are just calculated in percentages to show how much they increase the overall cost of the loan.

Mary and John decide to choose Bank ABC as their lender, since their APR shows that this bank charges the least in closing costs.

Now let's move on to the other boxes contained in the Truth in Lending statement.

2   **The finance charge** is what you will end up paying the lender for lending you the money.

3   **The amount financed** is the actual loan amount you are borrowing now and then paying back over 30 years.

4   **The total amount of payments** is the sum of the previous two items. This is the total amount you will be paying if you keep this mortgage for 30 years.

Mortgage Insurance

Most loans require mortgage insurance unless the borrower provides at least a 20 percent down payment. If you are putting down less than twenty percent, you must pay for mortgage insurance to protect the lender in case you default on the loan. It is a good idea to ask your loan officer how much monthly mortgage insurance you will be paying.

Escrow

To escrow means paying the amounts for homeowner's insurance, property taxes, and private mortgage insurance to the bank in your monthly housing bill instead of paying it directly yourself. The bank takes the responsibility of paying your taxes and insurance to the proper authorities.

Some buyers prefer not to escrow. They choose to pay property taxes and insurance on their own. If this is what you'd like, ask your loan officer if you have the option. Some types of loans require you to escrow. In most cases, banks will want you to escrow if you have a down payment of less than 20 percent.

Since many first-time homeowners find it harder to save up for separate tax and insurance payments that may be due twice per year in lump sums, for example, it is a good idea to escrow. It is more convenient for most to just pay similar amounts every month and have the bank coordinate where they go after that.

Money to bring to closing

You want to know how much money you will be required to bring to closing out of your own pocket. (Buyers who get grants to cover these costs may not have to bring anything).

Grants

Many homebuyers are eligible for grants, but they don't know it. Ask your loan officer if the lender participates in a down payment assistance program. If not, you will have to go to another lender if you want a grant.

Once you have a crystal-clear understanding of all these concepts and numbers, ask your loan officer to provide you with a **conditional pre-approval letter.** Make sure it is a pre-approval, not just a pre-qualification. They are different.

A pre-qualification letter is customarily provided to a borrower upon loan application, but no documentation has yet been submitted to the underwriter. A lender's underwriter is the final authority who thoroughly examines your documents and decides whether or not you will be approved for a loan. The evaluation you get from your loan officer is less substantial and more superficial than the one provided by the underwriter. Once the underwriter gives you a pre-approval letter, you have a better chance of getting a loan.

If you have had a successful meeting with your loan officer, you will feel pretty confident about moving along to the next step.

Step 8

Finding Out If You Qualify for Grants

A grant is different from a loan, since you do not have to pay it back. It is more like a gift—as long as you live in the home for a certain period of years (which could be anywhere from three to twenty or more). If you don't stay the required amount of time, you will have to pay some—or all—of the grant back.

Many first-time homebuyers are not aware that these grants are available. Those that do know about grants are often confused and misinformed. Sadly, consumers tend to have a negative perception of what homebuyer grants are and how they work. Many think they are hard to get, that you have to be poor to qualify, that they take a long time, that they are too complicated, that they ask you for too much paperwork, and they can get you into deep trouble.

Though some of these opinions are partly correct, most of them could not be further from the truth.

After having worked with grants for a number of years, I have become their greatest advocate. I cannot stress strongly enough the great opportunity they provide for many homebuyers.

If you are fortunate enough to qualify for grants (not everybody can), you could receive:

- $30,000 of grant money for those buying a home in a "Hope 6" area within the city of Houston, and who make up to 110 percent of Houston's "median house-hold" income. (Refer to glossary for definition). The Hope 6 areas included are: Near Northside, Settegast, Denver Harbor, Independence Heights, Acres Homes, Fifth Ward and Trinity Gardens.

- $19,500 if you buy a home within the city of Houston and make up to 80 percent of the "median household" income.

- $14,200 from Harris County if you buy a new house outside the city of Houston and within Harris County and make up to 80 percent of the "median household" income.

- $9,500 from Harris County if you buy a resale home less than ten years old outside the city of Houston, within Harris County, and make up to 80 percent of the "median household" income.

- Considerable sales price reduction, plus up to 6% of closing costs, if you buy a foreclosed home within a Neighborhood Stabilization Program. This program allows buyers to make up to 120 percent of the "median household" income.

- $14,500 from Southwestern Eastern Texas Corporation if you buy a new home in Austin, Baytown, Brazoria, Chambers, Deer Park, City of Dickinson, Galveston County, City of La Marque, City of La Porte, League City, Liberty County, Matagorda County, Pasadena, Shore Acres, Santa Fe, Texas City, City of Tomball, Waller County, Wharton County, Walker County Line (and some other locations) and make up to 80 percent of the "median household" income.

- $7,500 from Southwestern Eastern Texas Corporation if you buy a resale home in Austin, Baytown, Brazoria, Chambers, Deer Park, City of Dickinson, Galveston

County, City of La Marque, City of La Porte, League City, Liberty County, Matagorda County, Pasadena, Shore Acres, Santa Fe, Texas City, City of Tomball, Waller County, Wharton County, Walker County Line (and some other locations) and make up to 80 percent of the "median household" income.

- $19,500 from Southwestern Eastern Texas Corporation if you buy a home in the Sunset Meadow area in Pasadena and make up to 80 percent of the "median household" income.

- Considerable savings-matching money from Independent Development Accounts, as long as you buy a home that pays taxes to the city of Houston and qualifies through the Covenant Community Capital Corporation program. Income limits for this program are lower than 80 percent of the "median household" income.

- $15,000 from Home of Your Own if you purchase a home in Harris (outside the city limits of Houston), Montgomery, or Fort Bend Counties, at least one member of the household has documented disability, home built after 1978, and are below 80 percent "median household" income.

- Four percent of the mortgage amount, in the form of a two-lien, 30-year, 0% interest loan of Bond 77 money provided by the Texas Department of Housing and

Community Affairs. Though bonds are different from grants, since you do have to pay them back eventually, they are a good option for higher earners who cannot qualify for grants. For example, a family of three or more can qualify with a combined household income up to $76,935.

A couple of months ago, one of my clients got a $30,000 grant from the city of Houston to buy a house. He could barely believe he received so much so quickly. The grant took care of everything. He brought no money to the closing table at all. With his $30,000 grant, his monthly payments are only $623.90 a month.

Yes. $623.90 per month! Six hundred twenty three dollars and ninety cents a month for a new, $96,000 home with three bedrooms, two bathrooms, and 1300 square feet. Where can you get that in any part of the world?

And the $623.90 includes everything:

- ✓ Principal and interest
- ✓ Property taxes
- ✓ Mortgage insurance
- ✓ Homeowner's insurance

You may ask why the city and state would want to provide homebuyer grants to first-time homebuyers. Very good question:

It is known that homeownership stimulates the economy more than leasing does. When somebody becomes a homebuyer, he or she is obligated to pay property taxes—an important stream of income for federal, state, and city entities. To my mind, homebuyer grants and down payment assistance programs are, no doubt, a win-win solution for everybody.

Different grant programs have different guidelines and offer different amounts of money, depending on the geographical area where you will be buying a home, but there are some guidelines that programs tend to have in common:

1   **Income limits**: They are aimed at certain income brackets. You are disqualified if you make more than the allowed combined household income limit, but you'll need to verify where you fit into stated income limits.

    For example, let's say John and his wife Mary want to buy a home in the Near North Side of Houston, which is a Hope 6 area. John and Mary make a combined income of $40,000 per year, and they have two kids, ages nine and twelve.

www.homesatyourfingertips.com

John wants to see if he and his wife qualify for the $30,000 down payment assistance program provided by the city of Houston, so John goes to www.houstonhousing.org and checks a chart that looks similar to this:

Median Income Guidelines for 2013 in Houston, Texas

Family Size	80% "median household" income	110% "median household" income	115% "median household" income	120% "median household" income
1 person	$37,100	$51,040	$53,350	$55,650
2 people	$42,400	$58,300	$60,950	$63,600
3 people	$47,700	$65,560	$68,550	$71,550
4 people	$52,950	$72,820	$76,150	$79,450
5 people	$57,200	$78,650	$82,250	$85,850
6 people	$61,450	$84,480	$88,350	$92,200
7 people	$65,700	$90,310	$94,450	$98,550
8 people	$69,900	$96,140	$100,550	$104,900

John looks at the line in the first column for a family size of four. He also knows that for the particular home he wants to buy, his income cannot be over 80 percent of the "median household" income. On the chart, he sees that the most household income allowed for a family of four within the 80 percent bracket is $52,950.

At first sight, John and Mary do qualify for this program!

However, there might be more to qualifying than what appears on the surface, so I suggest you go straight to an experienced loan officer who specializes in grants and ask if you qualify.

Quick Note: Please be aware that median income levels do change and the guidelines are adjusted at least once a year.

2 **Loan Pre-approval**: You have to be preapproved for a loan with one of the participating lenders that works with grants.

3 **Number of years of residency**: You have to live in the home for a certain number of years. If you do not, and decide to sell the home before the specified time, you will have to pay back part (or all) of the grant.

4 **Savings**: The city and federal entities who provide the money require buyers to put some of their own money toward the home purchase. It really is not very much—maybe $350–$1,000—considering the amount of money you get from the program.

5 **First time homebuyer**: You do have to be a first-time homebuyer. This means that you cannot get grants if you already own a home (or owned one at any time within

the last three years). After three years of not owning a home, even if you had one before that, you are considered a first-time homebuyer again and can get a grant. You cannot get a grant to buy a second home. Needless to say, real estate investors cannot get grants.

6 **City home inspection**: The house needs to pass a home inspection. The grant program providers send their own inspectors to check whether the house is in good shape or not. If the house fails inspection, the grant will not be granted unless repairs are made. Please note that the grant inspectors check the home in addition to the inspector that you will hire (and the builder's inspector for a new home).

Properties that are dumps will most likely not pass inspection **AS IS**. Some first time homebuyers are willing to take the risk of paying for repairs before the house closes. However, make sure that grant authorities allow these repairs to be done before closing. Some might not permit it.

7 **Sales Price**: The sales price of the home you are buying has to be within a certain price range, but that range will vary from grant to grant.

8 **Neat documentation**: Your lender needs to provide specific, carefully packaged documentation to the grant entities. At this stage, sometimes a loan package

gets stuck in the pipeline because it is incomplete or was submitted incorrectly.

Once grant underwriters accept the package, they will check it over with a fine-tooth comb to make sure it follows all the necessary grant guidelines. If it does not, the loan officer usually must submit more documentation from the buyer to the underwriters until all questions are resolved. If all conditions are satisfied, the underwriter will provide a stamp of approval.

9 **Environmental inspection**: The grant authorities do an environmental report to make sure that the neighborhood where you want to buy the home follows environmental guidelines. For instance, if a home is near a landfill or in a high flood-zone area, it might not pass.

10 **Legal status**: The homebuyers need to have legal status in the United States. Buyers without legal status cannot qualify for grants even if they pay taxes.

11 **Mandatory HUD approved homebuyer class**: You have to take an eight-hour class with a Housing and Urban Development (HUD)-approved agency.

12 **Debt to income ratios**: Grant authorities, just like banks, check how much outstanding debt a buyer has in relation to income, which can affect qualification.

As mentioned in the previous chapter, this is called debt to income ratios. For more specific guidelines, please check the following websites:

- www.houstontx.gov/housing/homebuyer.html for homes within the city of Houston.

- www.sethfc.com/current_programs.htm for homes in Austin, Baytown, Brazoria, Chambers, Deer Park, City of Dickinson, Galveston County, City of La Marque, City of La Porte, League City, Liberty County, Matagorda County, Pasadena, Shore Acres, Santa Fe, Texas City, City of Tomball, Waller County, Wharton County, Walker County Line (and some other locations).

- www.hrc.hctx.net/dap.htm for homes outside of the city of Houston within Harris County.

- www.csd.hctx.net/ps_neighborhoodstabilizationprogram .aspx for foreclosed homes outside of the city of Houston and within Harris County (through the Neighborhood Stabilization Program). A foreclosed home is one that was repossessed by the bank when the owner stopped making mortgage payments.

- http://texashoyo.accesstexashousing.org/houston.htm for people with disabilities buying a home in Harris (outside of the city limits of Houston), Montgomery, or Ft. Bend Counties.

- www.covenantcapital.org for homes within the city of Houston. Covenant Community Capital Corporation offers independent savings account (as referred to in Step 4).

- http://www.tdhca.state.tx.us/homeownership/fthb/down-payment-assistance.htm if you are seeking bonds. The good news is that you just pay exactly what you borrowed.

- www.tdhca.state.tx.us/homeownership/fthb/mort_cred_certificate.htm. For homebuyers seeking Mortgage Credit Certificates (MCC) that allows claiming a tax credit for some portion of the mortgage interest paid per year. It is a dollar for dollar reduction against federal tax liability.

A few more comments about grants:

1 The consumer does not apply directly to the grant authorities; the lender initiates the grant process and stays in contact with the authorities. As noted earlier, your lender must participate in a given grant program for you to be able to use it.

2 Some grants are hard to combine with foreclosed properties (Not impossible, but difficult!).

3 Some down payment assistance programs can be combined as long as the money comes from different sources of funding. For example, I have seen homebuyers approved for $30,000 of grant money, plus Bond 77 money up to 6 percent of the home price, plus Covenant Community Capital Corporation savings-matching money.

4 I encourage all homebuyers to find a loan officer who specializes in homebuyer grants and can meet with you to explain how they work. As you have seen from the details in this chapter, getting a grant can be a complex, hard-to-understand procedure, but worth the effort.

5 Make sure you submit all the paperwork to the loan officer exactly as it is requested from you. Some times grant packages are turned down because the file was submitted improperly or incompletely. Keep in mind that you as a homebuyer will never be dealing with grant authorities directly. It is your loan officer who will be doing this. Therefore, it is important for your loan officer to be well acquainted with the guidelines each grant program requires.

6 Take an eight-hour home buying class with a HUD approved non-profit organization that covers in detail the down payment assistance programs. Try also meeting with a homebuyer counselor who is known to be very familiar with how the grant programs work.

Step 9
Meeting with a
Real Estate Agent

A real estate agent is the professional who will help you find your home.

In most real estate transactions, there are two agents:

1   The *buyer's agent* represents the buyer.

2   The *listing agent* represents the seller.

Though an agent is allowed to act as an intermediary between both the buyer and seller (in other words, there is only one agent working with both sides), it can get confusing.

Therefore, I recommend you choose just an agent who represents you as a homebuyer.

Be aware that one very common place where you are likely to meet a listing agent (who represents the seller) is when you visit an open house. The agent that you find hosting the open house is representing the seller. Many first time homebuyers do not know this, and get confused about who is representing who. I recommend you be perfectly clear of what type of representation you are getting as a homebuyer: It could be that your agent is representing YOU only, or it may be that you are getting dual representation and the agent is representing both buyer and seller at the same time (acting as an intermediary). Though this practice is legal in the industry, my experience is that it is difficult for a real estate agent to represent both parties at the same time and be completely fair and objective, especially when they have conflicting agendas.

There are many ways of finding a good real estate agent.

1   Asking friends and relatives

2   Visiting: www.har.com, the official site for Houston Association of Realtors.

3   Visiting www.trec.state.tx.us, which is the official site of the Texas Residential Real Estate Commission and checking real estate agent's credentials.

My best advice when choosing a real estate agent is to interview them in person (and not only through Facebook).

Buyers' agents, who represent only the buyer, customarily do not charge the buyer for their services. The agent is paid by the seller at the end of the transaction.

Whether they represent buyers or sellers, all agents are required to follow certain standards of ethics and best practices which are summed up in the acronym **OLDCAR**: obedience, loyalty, disclosure, confidentiality, accountability, and reasonable care.

Below is a list of standard activities that your agent should do for you:

● Find properties within your price range.

- Take you through the properties physically.

- Submit an offer on the standard forms provided by TREC (Texas Real Estate Commission).

- Negotiate an offer on your behalf with the listing agent (who represents the seller).

- Help you sign the contract with the seller.

- Make sure your earnest money and option fee are securely placed in an escrow account.

- Suggest that you hire a fully certified, licensed residential inspector.

- Maintain close communication with everybody involved in the process: loan officer, builder, inspector, appraiser, homeowner's insurance agent, title escrow agent, and so on.

I recommend that your agent also:

- Follow up with everybody and everything.

- Keep in close contact with you, the buyer, at all times.

- Be a smart and fair negotiator between both parties to get a win-win for everybody. (I call it the art of pushing/pulling/pushing/pulling).

- Keep cool despite any problems that arise.

- Be persistent and tenacious.

- Be a problem solver.

Whoever you decide to choose as your real estate agent, make sure you sign the following documents:

- Residential Buyer/Tenant Representation Agreement

- Information about Brokerage Services

- Broker Notice to Buyer Tenant

Step 10
Searching for a Home

Isn't this house beautiful?

Yes, it is, *but…*

The asking price is higher than what you can afford.

And the bank has only approved you for $100,000.

So **STAY WITHIN YOUR BUDGET!**

Now check this one out:

It's not as fancy as the other one, but, hey, it is a brand-new home with three bedrooms, two bathrooms, and is around 1300 square feet. It sold for $129,900.

And get this: the buyer got $30,000 of grant money from the city of Houston.

My point here is that Houston has unbelievable prices for beautiful homes—some of the best prices in the country! And it has fantastic home grants for those who qualify!

Why should you buy a home now?

Several reasons:

- As of 2013, we are in a buyer's market: There is a greater supply of homes than the demand of buyers ready to buy them.

- House prices are down, meaning that the same new house that was priced at $104,000 in 2006 can be bought now for $90,000.

- Interest rates are at an all-time low. (Go to www.bankrate.com to find current interest rates).

- Homebuyer grants are available for those who qualify.

What types of homes are out there?

- New homes

- Resale homes

- For-sale-by-owner homes

- Foreclosed homes

- HUD homes (foreclosed homes that were originally bought with FHA loans). Refer to glossary for definitions.

- Short sales

The reason I distinguish between these types of homes is that buying each type requires a different procedure:

1   **New homes** are mostly sold by builders. Builders write their own purchase contracts. With builders you have two options. You can build a customized home from scratch (it can take 3–6 months, depending on the weather, or you can buy an "inventory home" (new, but it already exists and you probably can't customize it).

> **Be aware** that just because a home is new doesn't mean it is perfect!

New homes are built by human beings and human beings make mistakes.

If you so decide to buy a new home, most likely your real estate agent will recommend to you to hire a Code Inspector. A Code Inspector holds the highest degree of inspection license in the country.

On rare occasions, builders discourage customers to spend money on an inspection, stating that it is not necessary. They claim that the house has already been inspected by city or county inspectors. Though this is true, to re-inspect the home is always a good idea, even if it is an added expense. Especially because this inspector, whom you hire, is looking out for your interests and can find problems in the home that the builder's inspector might have overlooked.

2   **Resale homes.** These are any homes that have already been lived in. When it's time to sell, the homeowner hires a listing agent to market the home. One of the most common places where sellers advertise their resale homes is in the multiple listing service. In Houston, it can be found at: www.har.com. Many of the asking prices of the homes listed in the MLS are a certain percentage higher than for which the seller would be willing to sell. This is done intentionally so that there is room for the price negotiation between buyer and seller.

3   **For-sale-by-owner homes**: These homes are sold directly from seller to buyer, usually with no real estate agent involved. However, buyers may want to hire their own agent to seek out adequate representation. If this happens, the homebuyer will have to pay the real estate agent's fee (since the seller is not willing to do so). These homes are listed at: www.forsalebyowner.com.

4   **Foreclosed homes**: Nowadays there are many of these available. As noted earlier, these are homes now owned by the lender who repossesses property when mortgages are not paid.

The process of buying a foreclosed home is different from the process of buying a resale home. Instead of agreeing to a contract with a seller, you bid on the property. Usually, the highest and best offer wins the bidding, so it is tricky. If your bid is lower than somebody else's, you will probably not win.

The process can also differ depending on who now owns the property. It could be: Freddie Mac, Fannie Mae, Chase Bank, Bank of America, Wells Fargo, or another lender. (Refer to glossary for definitions).

Foreclosed homes are generally sold at a discount, but they are normally sold *as is*, which means that the owner of the home is not willing to make any repairs. If you find a foreclosed home that is falling to pieces, it is unlikely that your lender will lend you money to buy it.

The home you buy will need to pass your lender's appraisal test. If the stove connections are pulled out, for example, it will not pass the appraisal guidelines. When you buy a home with a loan and a grant, it is not only the buyer that has to qualify for a loan (and pass many exams), but the property as well. In other words, if you qualify as a buyer, but the home fails to pass the inspection and appraisal test, you will not be able to buy it.

As I mentioned before, most foreclosed homes are very difficult to combine with grants (It is not impossible, but it is hard).

5 **Hud homes**: These homes are FHA foreclosed homes that are owned by the Federal Department, Housing and Urban Development. They generally are sold "as is," and at a discount. They have a pre-scheduled bidding period and there is no option period allowed.

HUD homes allow that earnest money be returned to the homebuyer for a variety of reasons, such as financing not pulling through, or an inspector finding home in less than a desirable condition.

HUD homes allow a certain percentage of seller's contribution, depending on the type of loan the previous owner had before the property was foreclosed.

HUD determines the number of days the homebuyer has to close, generally from 30-45 days. When going past this period, homebuyer is expected to pay an extra fee unless something else is negotiated with the seller, as needed, prior to each deadline. There are three extension periods allowed of 15 days each. Fees might be waived by HUD depending on each and every case.

HUD homes are difficult to combine with regular homebuyer grants or down payment assistance programs. However, they can be combined with bonds and mortgage credit certificates.

My suggestion with HUD homes is that you hire a knowledgeable real estate agent who is familiar of their guidelines and who can assist you during the process.

6   **Short Sales**: A short sale is a property where the owner owes more than the appraised value of the home. They also sell at a discount because the banks have agreed to take a loss and sell them for less than what the owner owes. How much less? Every case is different. Short sales usually take a long time to get approved by the bank.

With short sales, my biggest suggestion is: **have the patience of Job!**

Useful Questions to Ask Yourself While Searching for a Home:

● **Location**: Does the home have a good location? Does it have a chance of increasing in value within the next ten years? Though it is very hard to know in advance if the value of a home will increase or not in price, there are certain trends that can offer insightful information about projected property values. Just be aware that predictions based on statistical projections are most of the time only educated guesses. Nobody, not

even economy experts, knows for sure what will happen to property values in the future.

- **Schools**: Is the home near good schools? If somebody does not have children, this question might seem irrelevant to a homebuyer. However, it really is not. It is a known fact that good schools impact the quality of life in a positive way. They propitiate sound neighborhoods. On the same note, good neighborhoods with good schools are prone to charge higher property taxes. A good example of this in Houston is Katy.

- **Pride of ownership**: How do the neighbors take care of their lawns? Seems obvious, but it does say a lot about your neighbors' pride of ownership.

- **Safety**: What kind of activity is going on around the home at night? Is it quiet? Take a drive and check out the neighborhood. Are there rowdy bars, illegal activity, and shootings?

- **Flood zones**: Is the home in a flood zone?

- **Landfills**: Are there any landfills (garbage buried underground) near the home?

- **Property taxes**: What are the property taxes on the home? Remember that even if you pay off a 30-year loan, you will never stop paying property taxes.

- **Mud zone**: Is your home located in a MUD (Municipal Utility District)? This is a very important question to ask because it is an extra tax that you will have to pay to the county.

- **HOA regulations**: Is the home subject to Homeowners' Association regulations? If it is, how much will you have to pay per year? This is another mandatory expense. Some homeowners have lost their homes for not paying their HOA dues. Though many homebuyers focus on the drawbacks of HOA, there are also great benefits in having one: HOA help enforce rules and regulations that propitiate good neighborhoods with high standards.

- **Deed restrictions**: If your home has an HOA, what are its deed restrictions? Some homes are subject to extremely rigid regulations that you will have to follow. You might want to paint your house bright pink but not be allowed to do so.

- **Age of home:** How old is your home? Has it been well maintained? Has it been updated with energy-efficient appliances? If not, your light bill can add up to a lot. Ask the seller how much the electricity bill is during the hottest months of the year. Does the home have other energy-efficient features?

- **Age of appliances**: How old are all the machines in the home (such as the stove, heating, ventilator, air conditioner system, water heater, and so on)? Be aware that most machines have a certain life span.

- **Updates**: Have any of the systems of the home been reconditioned or updated (such as the electrical, plumbing, air conditioning system, the foundation, the roof)? When? How? With what materials? Who did the job? Could the seller provide you with any transferable warranties that the new homebuyer could use?

- **Foundation**: Does the home seem to have structural problems? Do you see cracks on foundation, ceilings or walls? Are there diagonal cracks above doors and windows? Slipping or shifted foundation? Floors that feel spongy or uneven? Inside doors or windows that don't fit? Be wary of recent paint jobs, especially those that might cover cracks.

- **Roof**: How old is the roof? Does it have more than one layer? Does it sag in the middle?

- **Water damage**: Does the home show signs of water damage? Look for stains on ceilings, moss and mildew on lower siding, and stains and mildew on underside of roof.

- **Home exterior**: In the outside, are there soggy areas in yard, eroded areas in walkway or driveway? Are there any signs of termites or ants? Is there old, flaky paint on sills or trim or exterior? Is siding spongy and wavy?

- **Building lines**: Does the home have building lines that are not straight? Walls that curve, windows or doors that look crooked or do not close properly.

- **Utility systems**: Are there any noticeable problems in utility systems? Are there very high heating or air conditioning bills? (ask to see bills). Is there leaking plumbing, especially the main water line? Make sure you turn on the water and look at the pipes. Is the main electrical service too small? (turn many lights and appliances on at the same time to see if they blow a fuse or circuit breaker). Are there any odd smells such as sewer gas? Is there lack of insulation in attic? (there should be thick insulation).

Do you remember the old proverb that says **not everything that glitters is gold?**

It's true!

On the same note, inquire about not only what you can see of the home, but what you do not see (the guts of the home, what is behind the walls).

Be extremely cautious when looking at a home, and extremely inquisitive. Do not be afraid to be a picky buyer.

And do not forget to look for a home within your budget!

Step 11

Submitting an Offer

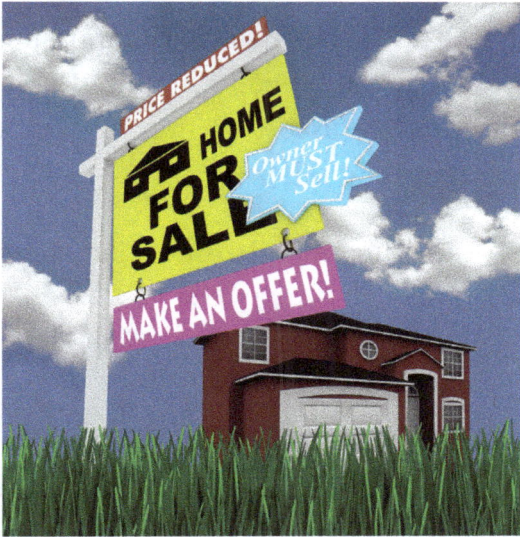

When you find a home within your price range that you like, the real estate agent who represents you submits an offer to the listing agent (who represents the seller). An offer is usually accompanied by earnest money, a kind of deposit to show your intention to completing the home-buyer transaction.

An offer is a written purchase proposal, or show of intent, that you put forward for the seller's consideration.

An offer only has the initials and signature of the buyer and doesn't become a binding contract until it is fully executed. "Fully executed" means that both sides have signed a contract, showing that they agree to everything it contains. An offer is not binding by itself.

The typical Texas Real Estate Commission standard boilerplate forms that are used to submit offers are exactly the same ones that are used to sign a fully executed contract between buyer and seller.

When an offer is submitted to the seller there are three possible outcomes:

1   The seller accepts it on the spot.

2   The seller presents a counteroffer that asks for a different sales price, closing date, closing costs, etc. It is common to negotiate back and forth several times with the seller.

3   The seller completely rejects the offer without making a counteroffer. You still have the right to submit a new offer that you hope will be more acceptable.

You may cancel your offer any time before the seller has signed it by telling your agent that you have changed your mind. Once the seller has signed the offer, your offer becomes a legally binding contract. If you break it, you could lose your earnest money or be sued by the seller for damages.

Keep in mind that if you submit a totally unreasonable offer, the chances of getting it accepted are low. Your real estate agent is key to providing you with sound common sense information.

The offer negotiation process is an art in itself. The good thing is that you do not have to do the negotiation. Your agent does it for you.

Sellers can do a few things to make it easier for buyers to buy, including:

- Paying for closing costs
- Paying for a homeowner's warranty
- Reducing the price of the home
- Making repairs on the home

Sometimes, homebuyers and sellers turn the negotiation process into an unproductive and stressful battleground of opinions. Not good!

Do carry out the negotiation courteously, respectfully, and professionally, so that you come to a win-win agreement.

If your realtor has experience negotiating offers and has a sharp antenna, he or she will have a good sense of what is possible and what is not.

Step 12

Signing the Contract

Here goes a quick "confession" question for you: Have you ever really read a contract carefully from beginning to end? I mean, any contract?

Be as honest as you can.

For example, did you read your credit card contract? Or your car loan contract when you signed up for financing?

I bet your answer is: **NO!**

Most of us do not read anymore…and even less often do we read contracts!

What many of us do nowadays is scan, skimp, skip, and scramble.

Have you ever wondered why?

1   We do not have enough time.

2   Reading legal contracts is not the most exciting thing in the world. We probably don't understand them even if we do read them.

3   We live in a fast-paced environment.

I suggest you take the time to read the contract—at least try to understand the main points. A good real estate agent will try to explain to you in simple language what the contract means, although they have to be careful, because it could be considered interpretation of the law, and they are not allowed to do that unless they are also lawyers. For legal questions, please consult an attorney.

Now, a very important point: I noted above that an offer is not binding, but a contract is.

"Binding" means that there is an expectation that both buyer and seller will perform every point of the contract and that both parties are held accountable for what they signed. If any of the parties decide to back out, there are consequences.

Therefore, be **EXTRA CAREFUL** to understand the terms of the agreement when you sign the contract.

Below are the major elements of the *One to Four Family Residential Contract (Resale)* promulgated by the Texas Real Estate Commission.

Please note that the order in which these elements appear in the contract do not reflect the order in which they happen in real life.

1   **Sales Price:** This is how much your home will cost—which is the amount the bank lends you plus the down payment you agree to pay up front.

2   **Financing:** This is what type of loan you are getting: fixed vs. variable, conventional vs. FHA or VA, and so on. (Refer to glossary for definition of terms). You'll need to be clear on the interest rate, how much your closing costs will be, and how much money you need to bring to the closing.

3   **Earnest Money:** Earnest money is a small amount of money that a seller asks a potential buyer to deposit in an escrow account before a home buying transaction is completed. An escrow account is a separate trust account where funds are held in the custody of a licensed financial institution for safekeeping until the end of the transaction. In Houston, when you sign a contract, you

are expected to put earnest money down to show the seller that you are serious about buying the property. The seller now can feel confident to take his home off the market and place it in pending status. Sometimes earnest money can create big problems when the homebuyer refuses to pay a small option fee that allows him to retract from the contract and get his earnest money back. Paying this small option fee can save you a lot of problems. Refer to paragraph 23 of the TREC *One to Four Family Residential Contract* to find where this information is written.

4   **Title Policy and Survey:** Once you have signed a fully executed contract between buyer and seller, the title company opens title and initiates an extensive title search examination. It reviews public records to determine the rights, liens, claims and other encumbrances that affect the property. Typical title issues could be claims such as fraud, forgery, alteration of documents, impersonations, secret marital status, incapacity of the parties, and errors in the public records known as hidden risks. If title is not free and clear, the seller will not be able to sell you his property. A title policy is a one-time expense that is part of the closing costs. Title insurance protects the homebuyer and the lender against any possible future title or ownership problems that could arise once the property has been purchased.

In Houston, sellers customarily pay for a buyer's title policy. However, everything in a contract is negotiable. Who pays for the survey (the map of the boundaries of the home)? Customarily, it is the buyer. Some sellers have kept their own survey and can provide it to you, saving you the expense of ordering another.

5   **Homeowners' Association:** Is the house you're buying in a community that has a Homeowners' Association? If so, what is its annual or monthly cost? What are its deed restrictions? For example, it may have rules against painting a house bright pink.

> Be aware that most new master communities charge HOA fees that are an added expense to the homebuyer.

6   **Statutory Taxes:** Yessiree, when you own a home, you have to pay taxes! If you don't, the bank can foreclose. It is a very good idea to ask your real estate agent how much the projected property taxes will be. Property taxes fluctuate depending on the appraised value that county authorities determine on a yearly basis. In Houston, Texas, the website to go to find public records of all properties in Harris county is www.hcad.org.

You have the right as a consumer to protest your property taxes in case you do not agree with the value imposed by the County. For more information go to: www.hcad.org.

7 **MUD Taxes:** MUD taxes can be an added housing tax expense that you might not have considered. Many new communities are in Municipal Utility Districts. This means that when the community was built, the developer borrowed money from the municipalities or the county via bonds. Guess who has to pay these bonds back? The homebuyers living in the community!

8 **Property Condition:** You want to be crystal clear whether you are accepting the property in its present condition or whether you want repairs done. If homebuyer notices that repairs need to be done in the home, these can be requested of the seller, via the seller's real estate agent. If seller refuses to do repairs, the homebuyer can always retract from the contract as long as an option fee has been paid, and the withdrawal is done within the option period. The seller is supposed to provide to homebuyer a copy of the Seller's Disclosure Notice. This is a document that discloses the seller's opinion of the condition of the property. This document is different from an inspection report that has the evaluation of an inspector.

9   **Closing Date:** Make sure you put in a reasonable closing date in the contract. Most transactions take from six to eight weeks to close, but if you are getting grants, it might take longer. Ask your loan officer for the estimated turnaround time for your loan to close.

10   **Possession of Property:** This is the time that you are provided with your keys, which is usually right after the seller has received the money for the home.

11   **Special Provisions:**

In this section you have the opportunity to ask the seller all kinds of special requests that are not indicated in other parts of the contract.

These requests can be as simple as asking the seller to remove the garbage found in his garage, or specific requests such as asking to reconnect utilities before inspection is scheduled. This section is also used to disclose relevant, unforeseen, non-typical circumstances that could delay or accelerate the home-buying process.

For example: the fact that the homebuyer is applying for grants. Sometimes these non-disclosed items can become the bone of contention between buyer and seller. Much of this can be prevented if open disclosures are clearly spelled out from the beginning. My advice is not to lie by omission, or try to hide uncomfortable information, that sooner or later will pop up and come out to haunt the homebuyer.

12 Settlement and Other Expenses: Do you know that you can ask the seller to contribute some money toward closing costs? This is the right time to ask. Don't be shy or afraid. Ask your real estate agent what amount is recommended for the seller to contribute toward your closing costs.

> Be aware that the amount of money that can be contributed towards closing costs is limited to a certain percentage of the sales price depending on the type of loan provided by the lender. While typically some conventional loans will only allow up to 3% of contribution of the seller, FHA permits up to 6% of seller contribution.

Keep in mind that many items of the contract are negotiable, even though you might not prevail. But you may try.

13 Mediation: If misunderstandings occur between buyer and seller during the transaction, there are two approaches to resolving differences: Mediation and arbitration. My take on this is to choose mediation over arbitration since the procedure towards resolution is friendlier, quicker and less cumbersome than that of arbitration (where everything is handled by a judge through a court procedure). If you choose mediation, the Texas Real Estate Commission assigns a mediator to settle differences.

14 Attorney's Fees: In the real estate transaction, attorneys are the professionals in charge of drawing final legal documents, for which they charge a fee for their services. This fee will be reflected in the HUD-1 or Settlement Statement that will be signed at closing. Be aware that if you so desire to hire an attorney to review the contract before closing, you have the right to do so, at your own expense.

15 Escrow: This paragraph sets forth both 1.) responsibilities as well as 2.) exclusions of liability of the escrow agent who is the assigned third party that acts as a middle person between buyer and seller. It also spells out how the earnest money will be handled whether the transaction is completed, or not completed.

16 Termination Option:

This paragraph is essential! An option fee is money you voluntarily pay a seller that allows you to back out of the contract if you wish to do so. I highly recommend that you pay for it, in order to have the option of retracting from the contract (within the option period), and not lose your earnest money. Since the **option fee** is voluntary, not mandatory, some buyers get tight and refuse to pay it. Not a good idea! I have known of buyers who lost their $1,000 of earnest money because they had not paid a $50 option fee.

I need to alert you that the option period is time sensitive. Be crystal clear as to starting and ending dates of the option period, and try to do your inspection during this time.

Step 13

Writing Your Earnest Money and Option Fee Checks

When you buy a home there are three kinds of expenses:

1   **Pre-closing Costs,** which the buyer generally pays before closing, and

2   **Closing Costs,** paid at the time of closing. (Some are paid by the buyer or a grant, some by the seller.).

3 **Down Payment Costs**, paid at the time of closing, and is the difference between the sales price and what the bank is willing to lend you. The earnest money check and option fee check is a pre-closing cost.

Once you and the seller have fully executed a contract, one of the first things you will have to do is to write an earnest money check payable to the seller's title company.

Two Quick Tips:

1 **Never write an earnest money check payable to a real estate agent.** It is illegal and can get you into a lot of trouble. And your agent can lose his or her license!

2 **Never give cash to anybody.** If you do not have a checking account, buy a money order and make a copy, and keep the copy in your records.

What is this earnest money all about? It provides the seller monetary proof and good faith that you are serious about buying the home.

The title company places the earnest money check in an escrow account, which protects the money and prevents anybody from fooling around with it. Only the escrow agent has administrative rights to disburse this money.

If the home-buying procedure flows smoothly, as we are hoping it will, the earnest money will be credited to buyer at the time of closing and applied toward the closing costs.

However, if Murphy's Law strikes and the transaction goes south, after the option period has passed, and if the earnest money terms are not clearly specified in the contract, who is entitled to the earnest money can become a big problem between buyer and seller. This is why I recommend home-buyers of being extra vigilant about understanding clearly when, where, and why you can have your earnest money returned to you if you decide to withdraw from the contract.

The option fee may or may not be credited back to the homebuyer at the time of closing. It depends which check box is marked in Paragraph 23 of the contract, so be sure to pay attention to Paragraph 23 before you sign.

As I have stated earlier, I have two pieces of advice regarding your earnest money and option fee:

1   It's better to pay a small option fee than to risk losing your earnest money should you wish to back out of the deal.

2   It is essential that you keep track of the exact days of your option period and not go past it.

Step 14

Meeting with Your Inspector

Once you have signed a fully executed contract and provided your earnest money check to the title company, the step to do immediately after, is to hire an inspector within the option period. This appointment is time sensitive. So please:

! Have the inspection done during this time. If the inspector finds major problems in the home that the seller is unwilling to repair, the homebuyer has the right to retract from the contract and get his earnest money back (as long as he paid an option fee to the seller). If homebuyer decides to withdraw from the contract after the option period, it is unlikely he will get his earnest money back (unless the contract is contingent of being preapproved by a bank and a grant).

Your inspector should be licensed by the Texas Real Estate Commission and should be known for being thorough. A Code Inspector is the highest inspector grade attainable.

The inspector will charge you for services at the time of inspection. You will need to pay out of your own pocket, and it is a nonrefundable fee. Inspection prices vary among inspectors and also depend on the square footage of the home. I have seen them range from $250 to $500.

An inspection is not mandatory (as are the appraisal, title insurance, and homeowner's insurance). However, it is very much recommended! Some homebuyers refuse to get an inspection just to save money. Their logic is: "Why should I hire an inspector if I can have my brother-in-law look at the house? He has worked in construction all his life and is so capable. He can do it for me for the price of a lunch!"

No offense to your brother-in-law, but unless he is a trained home inspector, he does not know the inspection code and won't know what to look for.

And please, attend the inspection yourself! You will learn a lot. Bring a pad, a pen and a few pencils to take notes, and ask lots of questions.

If you are buying a new home, don't think you do not need to hire a licensed inspector. You do! New homes, though they can look perfect, are often not. Human beings who make mistakes build them. Not only should you hire a licensed inspector if you buy a new home, but a code inspector as well. The code inspector has achieved the highest degree in this field.

> Make sure you do the inspection during the option period, and not after you have closed on your home!

There are several types of inspections. The most common are:

- Technical and mechanical

- Termite

- Lead inspection for homes built before 1978.

At a minimum, your inspector will look at the:

- **Foundation**: What kind of foundation does the home have? Is there enough slab exposure in the home? Has it settled? Does it have cracks? Keep in mind that the presence of cracks is not necessarily a bad sign. Some homes have cracks but have not settled. Others do not have cracks, but have settled. In Houston, Texas, the soil is clayish, not rock-solid as in San Antonio or New York. This means that most Houston foundations are built with post-tension cables that allow for homes to float and avoid settling.

- **Drainage**: Is grading/drainage system in place? Does it drain away from the structure? Are partial gutters and downspouts in place?

- **Roof**: What type of roof does the home have? How old is the roof? What is the useful life of this roof? Has the roof been changed? If it has, how long ago? To save themselves the expense of replacing the whole roof, some sellers pay a minimum amount to add a layer of shingles to the existing layers. Building code law allows for no more than two layers on the same roof. More than two will put a lot of weight on the structure.

- **Attic** and **insulation**: Does the wood framed roof have all the components it should have? Is there presence of a cat walk? Is attic ventilation operating properly? (soffit vents, ridge vents and fixed roof ventilators?)

- **HVAC system:** HVAC stands for *heating, ventilator, air conditioning system*. The HVAC system has a lot of components (furnace, heat exchanger, ducts, compressor, condenser, and air conditioner). The inspector will check that the HVAC is fully operational. You want to ask your inspector if these elements have been maintained properly and whether there are any leaks in the HVAC. Leaks can become a major issue, especially if carbon monoxide (the silent killer) is escaping. Keep in mind that the system not only controls the inside temperature of the home but is also responsible for controlling the purity of the air you breathe.

- **Windows:** Are windows and window screens in sound condition? Are they in place? Are they fully operational? What type of windows does the home have? (double-paned or single-paned?) Do they have argon in them? Are they energy efficient? Energy efficient windows will help you save on your electric or gas bills.

- **Electrical system:** What kind of electrical box does the home have? Are the breakers labeled? Are circuit breakers the correct size and connections tight? Are arch fault circuit protectors in place? Are ground rod, clamp and ground wire in place and tight? Are connections well installed? What type of wiring is used (copper, aluminum, or something else)? Has the electrical system been updated? Has the electrical box been wired properly? Is the electrical system grounded properly? Does home have properly functioning GFCIs (ground fault circuit interrupter) in wet areas of the home? GFCIs protect homeowner from electrical shock when being near water areas such as bathrooms, kitchen, and spas.

> Ask seller how much he pays on electrical bills during the hot summer months.. In some older homes that have no energy-efficient features, the bill can add up to a lot of money—sometimes as much as a mortgage payment. Be careful. Pay attention.

- **Gas system:** What is the condition of the gas system in the home? Are pipes properly installed? Is there any gas leakage?

- **Plumbing and drainage systems:** What types of water pipes does the home have? Are they fully operational? How old are they? Have they been updated? Are there any leaks? How is the drainage system of the home working? Is there enough water pressure in the home? Water outside should flow away from the home, not toward it. Is there any evidence of mold in the home? Ask your inspector where all the shut off water valves are located.

- **Water heater**: How old is it? Is water heater pan in place? Does the drain line terminate to the outside? Is a galvanized gas line, flex line and gas shut-off valve in place? Is vent pipe in place and strapped. Is T & P relief valve and positive gravity flow discharge line in place and is it terminated to the outside?

- **Appliances:** How have all the machines in the home been maintained? Are they operating properly? Inspector checks that dishwasher, food waste disposer, range exhaust vent, ranges, cooktops, ovens and microwave oven work properly.

- **Walls:** What kinds of materials are the walls made out of? (sheetrock, plaster, etc.). How have the walls been maintained? Are they in sound condition? Do they have any cracks?

- **Ceilings and floors:** Are they in sound condition? Do they have cracks, sloping and water stains?

- **Siding** of the home: What kind of materials is the exterior siding of the home made of (Hardie Plank, brick, wood, metal)? Have they been properly maintained? Do any of the materials have a warranty?

- **Landscaping:** Though the inspector is not obliged to check things such as weeds, the type of grass, or the pH of the soil (unless they affect the proper functioning of the home), it is a good idea to find out more about the landscaping, especially whether the drainage flows toward or away from the house. Sometimes trees with deep roots can cause major structural damage and shifting of the foundation of the home.

There are lots and lots of components to a home, so we have only covered a few here.

A quick note about inspectors and inspector reports:

An inspector is not a soothsayer or a prophet. He cannot know what will happen in the future of the home. However, an inspector should be able to theorize about what is behind the walls from any visible, telltale signs. You will notice on most property inspection reports a clause stating that an inspection might not reveal all deficiencies. A real estate inspection helps reduce some of the risk involved in purchasing a home, but it cannot eliminate these risks, nor can the inspection anticipate future events or changes in performance due to changes in use or occupancy.

Step 15

Understanding Title Insurance

Very soon after you sign the contract, and your real estate agent submits it to the title company together with the earnest money, the title company will immediately begin what is called a title search.

A title search is an extensive investigation of the property you plan to buy, checking if there are any liens, claims, title or ownership issues. Title is another word for ownership of the property.

You will be receiving in the mail a copy of your title insurance policy, title search, and tax information.

Read it Carefully!

The purpose of this title search is to investigate the chain of title and give you a history of who owned your home, so you can be sure that the person selling you the house really has the right to do so. It ensures the lender and the homebuyer that the title is free and clear. If it is not, title issues need to be resolved by seller before closing. Otherwise seller will not be able to sell you the home.

Usually the person who holds title to the property is the person whose name is on the deed. However, there are issues that can cloud a title or make it difficult to know who owns the property.

A title officer or escrow agent, who is the person who will be doing the title investigation, works for a title insurance company that sells insurance to guarantee that the title report is accurate and that you can rely on it. All lenders require the buyer to pay for a lender's policy of title insurance up to the amount of the mortgage. This protects the lender if there is an error in the title report. There is also an owner's policy of title insurance to protect the buyer's ownership share of the home.

In addition to finding title issues during the home-buying transaction, title policies also offer the only protection available against hidden defects of title which might appear after closing, and were not discovered during the home buying process. These future title problems could be forgery, impersonation, capacity of parties, faulty acknowledgements and unpaid material and mechanic liens.

Typical title issues:

1   The seller may lack title to the property because of a problem in the chain of title, or unbeknownst to him/her, may not own all of the interest in the property he has the intention of selling.

2   Claims against the property (for instance, if the owner was sued and a judgment was attached to the property).

3   Tax money the owner has not paid.

4   A mechanic's lien (placed against the property if the owner didn't pay a contractor).

5   Ownership issues: For example, when somebody shows up as an owner who nobody suspected was the owner, or when there are no written records stating who has legal title of ownership to a property.

Who pays for title insurance?

In Houston, Texas, the seller customarily pays for title insurance, although this can be negotiated in a contract. Title policies tend to cost around 1 percent of the home's sales price.

Step 16

Undertanding Your Residential Appraisal

Evaluation

☑ OUTSTANDING

☐ Excellent

☐ Very Good

☐ Average

☐ Below Average

Soon after the inspection is done, the lender sends an appraiser to estimate the value of the home you want to buy. Based on the results of the appraisal, the lender will decide how much to lend the borrower.

Customarily, the banks or lenders are the ones who choose the appraiser. However, if homebuyers want to have a say as whom the appraiser will be, they can certainly do so. Keep in mind though that this appraiser will need to be approved by the lender.

The most frequently and accepted method of doing a residential appraisal is called the sales comparative approach. It consists of comparing the home you want to buy with other similar homes in the neighborhood that have sold in the past six to twelve months. The appraiser will make a final determination of how much your home could be sold for in the current market.

If the house appraises for less than the contract price, the bank will only lend you the amount for which it was appraised. No more.

In such a case, there are two ways to proceed:

1   The seller can accept a lower sales price to match the appraised value.

This is the recommended approach!

2   If the seller does not want to lower the price of the property and the homebuyer wants it badly enough, then homebuyer can pay the difference between the appraised sales price and the appraised value.

This is not smart! Not recommended!

However, if the appraised value turns out to be higher than the sales price, you are ahead of the game! You already have equity in your home.

Equity is the difference between the value of the house and what the seller/owner owes on the house.

Please ask your lender for a copy of the appraisal report as soon as it is completed. By law, you have the right to get one.

The appraisal report is ready for you very soon after the inspection is completed.

On most occasions, the homebuyer pays for the appraisal before closing, so it is one of those "pre-closing" costs.

! Be careful about getting carried away about the home you want to buy.

If the house you happen to have chosen as your dream home appraises for less than the sales price, don't pay the difference! Be coolheaded about it, even if you have fallen in love with the house and want no other. Ask the seller for a price reduction.

If the seller refuses, **think twice** whether you want to buy the property. The property may be worth less than what the seller is asking for, and it might not be as valuable as you think it is.

Ask the lender for a copy of your appraisal report before you buy your home. Don't wait until closing.

Always remember that appraisals are safety valves for homebuyers. They protect you from paying more for a home than the home is worth. Your property should be in the same range as others in the area.

Step 17
Understanding Your Survey

One of the items that will be required by the lender and title company when you buy a home is a survey.

A survey is a property sketch, diagram or map of the home you want to buy that indicates legal boundaries, easements, encroachments and rights of way of the property you are buying.

A surveyor is the professional in charge of doing the survey. He generally is a licensed engineer who stakes the boundaries of the property you will be buying and creates a scale drawing that shows the location of the residence, fence lines, and improvements that have been made to the property (such as a patio or garage) to be sure that they do not encroach on an adjoining property.

A surveyor's greatest skills are:

- Measuring the boundary lines of a property with maximum precision and exactitude
- Not to overlook anything that should be included in the survey
- Being as thorough as possible.

Title company or lender generally orders the survey, soon after the title investigation is completed.

If you would like to suggest a surveyor of your liking, you can certainly do so. However, he/she will need to be approved by the bank and the title company.

If you are buying a resale home, the seller is likely to be able to provide you with an existing survey, so that you do not have to pay for another. If this is the case this survey needs to be certified by the title company as a true legal

document. The validity of a survey depends on it being a comprehensive reflection of the property in its current state.

If the seller does not have a survey, if the survey is more than ten years old, or if it is outdated (for example, if an addition was made to the home that was not marked in the previous survey), a new survey will have to be made.

If a new survey has to be ordered, ask your title company when the surveyor will be going out to the property and then attend the survey. It is much easier to understand what the diagram of a survey means while walking physically through the property alongside with the surveyor, than later on at the closing table, when you will only be able to see the survey on paper.

If seller has provided you with a survey, take your time and re-visit the home you want to buy to check survey items. Be clear on the boundary lines of your property and any encroachments, easements, or setbacks. Check whether your home is in a flood zone.

Surveys tend to be one of the most overlooked and under-explained legal documents in the whole home-buying transaction process.

It is to your advantage to know exactly how much land you are paying for and to identify defects or problems in the demarcation of boundary lines of the property that are not easily identified on the property (if there are any) and that could become an issue in the future.

If the survey shows defects in the property, you might be able to renegotiate the price of the property.

Generally the buyer pays for the survey as part of the closing costs, unless a different arrangement is made with the seller prior to signing the purchase agreement. That is, the survey fee is a negotiable item within the contract.

My experience as a real estate agent is that many buyers do not pay much attention to the survey, and generally get it at the very end, at the closing.

This is not good.

Survey issues can become big issues!

I recommend you to try to get the survey within the option period—or at least, way before the closing. If this is not possible, you should insist on visiting the property, walking through it, and getting a pretty good sense of four elements of the survey: boundary lines, encroachments if any, easements if any, and whether the home is in a flood zone.

Let's define these four elements:

1   **Boundary lines**: These include property lines and setback lines or building lines. A setback line is the distance from the property line or other established line within which no buildings may be constructed. A setback line is established by municipal authorities that determine the points beyond which no building may extend to ensure that streets will appear uniform.

2   **Encroachments**: An encroachment occurs when a home or other element (such as a pool, a shed, a fence, or shrubbery) extends out from one property onto another, across property lines.

When the property you want to buy invades your neighbor's property (or the other way around), you cannot simply remove an encroachment even if you want to. Both encroacher and encroachee have rights, and they need to discuss them.

3   **Easements**: These are public rights-of-way located on your property. Third parties, such as utility companies, have rights to do things on otherwise private land. In other words, if the surveyors find an easement on your property, this means you are granting somebody else legal rights to use your land (usually only the specific part of it shown on the survey). The most common

easements are granted to utility companies to run power lines and cable. However, you may also grant an easement to your neighbor—for instance, to cross your property if it blocks his access to a road.

If easements are not marked on the survey it is important to have them added. These may represent potential litigation issues in the future.

4   **Flood zones:** If you see a mark indicating Zone B, C, or X, in the survey, it is a Non-Special Flood Hazard area. In those zones there is no immediate danger from flooding from overflowing rivers or hard rains. However, the letter A indicates that your property is in a Special Flood Hazard Area. Such a home has a greater chance of suffering flood damage during the term of a 30-year mortgage; in that case the bank will require you to get flood insurance.

If you want to know if the property you are buying is in a flood zone in Houston, Texas, go to: www.tsarp.org

In some homes in Houston where soil is known for its unstable properties, an elevation survey is sometimes a good thing to do. A foundation elevation survey shows how level or out of level the foundation is now.

Step 18

Meeting with a Homeowner's Insurance Agent

If you have gone this far in my book, you have probably noticed that you may already have been required to purchase two types of insurance:

1   Private mortgage insurance and
2   Title insurance

There is another required insurance policy:

3 Homeowner's insurance.

And if the home is located in a flood zone:

4 Flood insurance will also be required.

Homeowner's insurance isn't a luxury. It's a necessity. In fact, most mortgage companies won't make a loan until the buyer provides proof of coverage. Homeowner's insurance protects you if the home suffers a fire, windstorm damage, or theft, or causes a third party injury, and so on.

Homeowner's insurance can be very expensive. Those that live in high-risk areas—close to major waterways or known earthquake fault lines—will pay the most. In fact, they are often forced to pay annual premiums in the many thousands of dollars. But after Hurricane Ike, average insurance premiums went up even for homeowners in relatively sedate, suburban neighborhoods.

The amount of coverage you want is completely up to you. In 2010, a Texas law was passed stating that mortgage companies cannot require the homeowner to carry coverage for the full value of the property (most of the time, this is determined by purchase price).

I have seen buyers do three different things:

1   Getting basic insurance (buying the bare minimum required by the bank to get a loan).

2   Getting a little more than the minimum.

3   Getting too much insurance.

I recommend that a buyer be on the safe side. Get a little more than the basic policy, but not so much that it strips your pocketbook.

Here are some useful pointers and questions to ask your insurance agent:

Coverage

What items does my homeowner's insurance cover?

Most homeowner's insurance policies break the property coverage into four sections:

1   *Coverage A*: The home

2   *Coverage B*: Detached structures

3   *Coverage C*: Contents (personal property)

4   *Coverage D*: Additional living expenses

Depending on the type of homeowner's policy, the perils covered will vary. For example: HO-1 is a basic form of insurance and covers a limited amount of perils. HO-2 adds more perils and HO-3, the most popular, covers all perils except those that are excluded (like flood, earthquake, war, nuclear attack).

Deductible

As you might very well know, most insurance policies require a deductible. This means that if you have a claim, you will have to pay out of your own pocket until the deductible is satisfied. The formula that applies here is: the larger the deductible, the lower the insurance premium.

Replacement costs versus actual cash value

Most people want their property replaced after it is damaged. There are two possibilities of what type of coverage you can get:

- **Actual Cash Value:** If you experience a loss when your home is insured under the actual cash value option, the insurance company will pay you only the amount of money for the *depreciated* value of your home, not its *market* value. Depreciated value refers to the wear and tear of the home due to its age. This means that the insurance company doesn't give you enough money to cover all your expenses and you'll pay a substantial amount out of your own pocket.

- **Replacement Cost:** With this option your insurance agency will pay the total amount it would cost you to rebuild your home less the policy deductible. In most cases, replacement costs exceed actual cash value. Replacement cost is more expensive since it has better coverage in cases of loss.

  Replacement costs only apply if you insure your dwelling for at least 80 percent of its full replacement cost. If your insurance falls below the required percentage, then actual cash value will be used.

5 **Liability protection against third parties**: It covers payment to third parties who sue you for acts they hold you liable or responsible for. In addition to liability insurance, your policy will include medical payment coverage if somebody is hurt or suffers some kind of injury while being at your home.

The cost of the insurance premium

This depends on several factors:

1 **Your credit score:** Some insurance agencies will pull your credit before issuing a policy. If you have a lower credit score your premiums may be higher.

2 **Type of construction:** Type of construction and quality of the type of materials used to build the home (brick, wood, hardi-plank). Some homes are built on a more solid foundation than others and can stand up better to perils.

3 **Condition of the house:** If an older home's wiring has been changed and other improvements have been made, premiums will go down.

4 **Location of the Home:** If the home is in a hurricane, earthquake, or a flood zone, your premium will be higher.

5 **Geographic loss experience:** If a lot of claims have been filed in a certain geographical area, and the insurance company has lost a lot of money in your area, premiums rise regardless the quality of your home.

6 **Proximity to the nearest fire hydrant** and 24 hour man fire station may lower your insurance rates.

7 **Type of fire protection:** If you have a volunteer fire department rather than a professional one, your rates can be higher.

8 **House size:** the bigger the house, the more it will cost to replace the damaged material. Therefore, cost of insurance may be higher.

9   Alarm system: If your home has an alarm system, you can get a discount.

10 Age of home: If the home is old, and not well maintained, your insurance most likely will be higher.

11 New home insurance is discounted.

If you have good credit and choose a comprehensive plan that includes all your insurances under one policy (car, property, life insurance), you can get a discount.

Flood Insurance

If you are in a flood zone, you will be required to get flood insurance. If you are not in a flood zone, but near one, you might want to consider buying flood insurance while it is still affordable.

If some time in the future your home becomes part of a flood-prone area, you will be required to buy it and it will cost you more.

Think twice before buying a home in a flood zone. Not only because you will have to purchase extra flood insurance that will raise your monthly housing expenses, but because having to move out of your home is always a hassle if your home gets flooded.

Think ahead, NOW. The stress of seeing your home in shambles is avoidable!

Interestingly enough, I have noticed that some homes in a flood zone have never flooded, while other homes that are not in a flood zone have.

If you want to know if the property you are buying is in a flood zone, go to: www.tsarp.org

Quick alert about **insurance:**

If a hurricane approaches Houston while you are in the process of buying a home, most insurance agencies will put a hold on providing homeowner's insurance until the hurricane passes. Obviously, this can delay your purchase process.

Step 19
The Closing

You have found your dream home, signed a purchase agreement with the seller, and have been approved for a mortgage. Now it's time to close the deal!

The closing completes the real estate sale and the mortgage loan transaction. At the closing, you'll have to review and sign a number of documents to complete the closing process. You might feel overwhelmed by the stack of documents presented to you, but you should always feel free to ask questions to the closing agent. Your home will probably be your largest asset, and you should be comfortable signing each document pertaining to its purchase.

Below are a few suggestions to prepare for a closing:

Do a final walk-through inspection two days before the closing to make sure that the house is in sound condition.

Get a copy of your settlement statement which shows all the costs of the sale and who pays for them. It will tell sellers how much money they will get at closing and tells you how much money you need to close.

If you are married, bring your spouse (Texas is a community property state and both spouses need to be at the closing table). You (and your spouse, if any) should bring photo identification (such as a driver's license).

Bring a cashier's check made out to the title company if you will be making a payment. Your real estate agent will inform you the amount of money you need to bring to closing. If it is more than $500.00, most title companies will require you to bring a cashier's check made to the attention of the title company. Some buyers that receive grant money do not have to bring anything to closing (the grant pays for everything).

Always make sure you understand what you are signing.

Don't hesitate to ask for a five-minute break to refresh your brain cells!

Since you will not have time to read all the documents you initial and sign, at least make sure you understand the most important ones:

1   **The HUD-1 or Settlement Statement**: HUD stands for Housing and Urban Development. The HUD-1 is generally one of the first documents that the escrow agent will explain to you in a lot of detail. The HUD-1 contains a break down of all expenses involved in the purchase of your home.

Homebuyers need to be aware that the figures appearing in the HUD-1 need not vary much from the figures of the Good Faith Estimate provided by the loan officer at the beginning of the home-buying process. By law there is a certain percentage of difference allowed. Check with your loan officer what that percentage may be.

Closing costs typically average between 3 and 7 percent of the sales price of the home, depending on when and where you purchase your home. Your down payment is also paid at closing.

The HUD-1 is divided into two columns: one lists what the buyer pays, and the other lists what the seller pays. All costs and fees associated with the transaction for both the buyer and seller will be there, including the purchase price, earnest money deposit, loan fees and costs, mortgage payoffs for the seller, commissions to real estate agents, title charges, escrow amounts, and the amount you will need to bring to closing (if any) to purchase the property and close the transaction.

Your loan officer or real estate agent should review the HUD statement with you prior to closing so that you are not caught off guard by any costs or fees in the statement. Even so, you should still review the HUD statement carefully at the closing and take your time and express your questions or concerns, if any. Give yourself time to go over this document comfortably. A HUD-1 can be confusing, so don't be shy about asking questions. Also, please be aware that often mistakes can be made and they should be corrected.

2 **Promissory Note**: This lays out the terms under which you promise to pay your loan: how much you will have paid in total after the end of the loan term, what your interest will be, the terms and place of payment, the type of loan, the monthly payment amount, your right to prepay the loan, what will happen if you fail to pay your obligations under the note, the first date you are expected to pay your first payment, and so on. The promissory note is secured by your signature on a Deed of Trust (see below).

3 **Final Federal Truth in Lending Disclosure Statement:** This document is often confusing for homebuyers, especially first-time buyers. It sets forth your loan amount, your interest rate, and the annual percentage rate (APR). The APR includes the quoted interest rate on the loan plus all additional service and finance charges associated with the loan, including those paid at the time of closing and those paid over the term of the loan. The APR is usually slightly higher than the note's interest rate. The Truth-in-Lending is required by federal law and is designed to protect consumers by giving a clear disclosure of the terms and costs of the loan.

Make sure you compare the initial APR figure of the first Truth in Lending, provided to you by your loan officer at the beginning of the process, with the final APR of the Truth in Lending presented to you at the closing table. The figures should be similar, or they should not vary much, one from the other, unless closing costs increased dramatically.

4   **The Deed of Trust**: This is a lengthy legal document that pledges real property to secure the loan. It recognizes your ownership of the property but gives the lender the right to claim the property if you fail to meet the terms of the note. It establishes your rights and obligations regarding your mortgage. The Deed of Trust will show a detailed legal description of the property you are purchasing and confirms that you are pledging it as collateral for repaying the loan, which means that if you do not make your loan payments as set forth in the promissory note, the lender may foreclose on the property and sell it to pay off your loan.

5   **The General Warranty Deed with Vendor's Lien**: This document conveys transfer of ownership of title from the seller to the buyer and is usually signed only by the seller. It records the name, address, and phone number of the buyer and seller, the legal description of the property, the contract date, and the contract purchase price. The form is used by local assessing officials and the state for a variety of purposes. Please note that this deed will be recorded by the county. Expect to

receive the original in the mail two to six weeks after you close on your home. Do not throw it out!

6   **Escrow Statement**. This document will set forth the items escrowed into your monthly mortgage payment if you choose to escrow items such as your homeowner's insurance and your county taxes. Doing so means that a certain amount of your monthly payment will be placed in an escrow account so that the lender can pay the taxes and insurance when they become due.

7   **Survey**: Contains the map or boundaries of the property you are buying, and all structures and important features of the property.

8   **Title Insurance**: Protects the lender and the home-buyer against any title defect, such as liens or other claims against the property.

9   **Title Abstract:** It is a summary of the public records that relate to the ownership of the property and a history of the property's ownership.

10 **Affidavits**: Documents that validate certain information in writing and will vary according to your situation.

11 **Property Tax Exemptions Form**. This document shows different tax exemptions you could qualify for now that you have purchased a home. If you will be living in this home as your primary residence, you will

qualify for a homestead exemption. If you don't receive this form at closing, you can download it yourself from www.hcad.org.

Depending on the lender and its requirements, there are often other loan documents to be executed than those I have listed. In addition, the real estate agents and the title company might have several documents for you to execute.

If you are presented with any of these legal documents before closing, take advantage of the opportunity to read as much of them as you possibly can ahead of time.

Don't be shy about asking your escrow agent questions.

Now, there are a few important things to take care of after you buy your home that will be covered in the last chapter of this book.

Step 20

Now that You are a Homeowner, What's Next?

The journey of buying your home has ended. However, now begins the most exciting part: How to maintain your home in the best possible shape, and how to protect your valuable investment.

Immediately after you close on your home do the following:

- Put all your new home's utility bills into your name. Try doing it before the previous owner shuts you off.

- Call the city to request a garbage can and recycle bins, and find out your garbage day pickup dates (call 311).

- Make sure you file for Homestead Exemption (you will get a discount in property taxes).

This is customarily done the year after you have bought a home.

Quick Note! You do not need to pay anybody to do this for you. Do it yourself by filling in the blanks of the *Residential Homestead Exemption* form that can be downloaded at www.hcad.org. It can take you about fifteen minutes to complete. Then send it in the mail or go directly to the Harris County Appraisal District offices and deliver it yourself. You will get from 18 to 20% discount of your property taxes if the home you have bought is your primary residence.

- Pay your mortgage on time!

- If you have Homeowners' Association fees, pay them on time.

- If you haven't done so already, get the Homeowners' Association's Deed Restrictions to get a clear picture of what you can and can't do in case you decide to remodel, build onto, or make any kind of changes to your home.

- If you have difficulty paying your mortgage because you lose your job or have any other problem, seek help! There are a lot of nonprofit organizations that can provide free counseling.

- If you bought a new home, make sure you know what your warranty covers and for how long. Be advised that all warranty policies are not iron clad.

- Be a proud owner. Always maintain your home in excellent shape.

- Enjoy your wonderful investment!

I hope this book has served its purpose: to be a useful guide to you and your loved ones.

I congratulate you on your home buying journey, and wish you all the best in your future endeavors as a proud home-owner!

Appendixes

Costs of Buying a Home

How much did it cost John to buy a $96,000 home in February, 2012?

Pre-closing Costs

Credit pull	$11.91
Appraisal	$470.00
Homebuyer's class	$15.00
Earnest money check	$500.00
Option fee check	$100.00
Inspector	$375.00
Total	**$1471.91**

John paid **$1471.91** out of his own pocket **before** closing.

Closing Costs

Closing costs can range from 3 to 7 percent of the sales price. Some of these costs are negotiable; some are not.

Below you will find listed some closing costs that come from a real transaction:

Origination charge for lender	$1,190.00
Mortgage insurance premium	$690.00
Homeowner's insurance for one year	$677.00
Daily Interest	$68.76
Settlement or closing fee for title co.	$250.00
Owner's title insurance	$911.80
Lenders title insurance	$225.00
Tax certificate from title	$64.95
Tax service fee	$105.00
Messenger	$50.00
Attorney for document preparation	$50.00
Government recording charges	$130.00
Deed	$30. 00
Mortgage	$100.00
Releases	$30.00
Survey	$378.88
Reserves homeowner's insurance (3 mos.)	$169.25
Reserves city property taxes (5 mos.)	$861.85
TOTAL	**$5,982.49**

Do you know how much the buyer paid of the $5,382.49 at the closing table?

Nothing!

The $30,000 grant money covered it all!

Do you know how much he is paying per month in housing expenses?

$623.90 per month. With everything included!

Monthly Housing Expenses Breakdown

Principal and Interest	$332.71
Homeowners Insurance	$56.42
Private Mortgage Insurance	$62.40
Property Taxes	$172.37
Total	$623.90

Who Does What While You Are Buying a Home?

Homebuyer Instructor

- Works for a nonprofit community development corporation.

- Teaches you all the steps involved in buying a home.

- Provides you with easy exercises and examples to make the home buying process easier to understand.

- Most homebuyer instructors provide an eight-hour Housing and Urban Development (HUD)-approved class and a certificate of attendance.

Homebuyer Counselor

- Works for a nonprofit community development corporation.

- Meets with you to see where you are and where you need to go regarding the home buying process.

- Provides useful and insightful information that will help you evaluate your options and make intelligent decisions regarding your home purchase.

- Offers credit rebuilding support and budget assistance to strengthen financial healthful habits.

- Most homebuyer counselors are very knowledgeable about grants.

Loan Officer

- Works for the lender.

- Pulls credit. I recommend you pull your own, although lender will want to pull it again.

- Takes loan application to see what your chances are of being approved for a loan.

- Explains to you the terms of the loan, the interest rate, the closing costs, and so on.

- Works directly with grant officials from the down-payment assistance programs.

Loan Processor

- Works for the bank.

- Checks to see if your documents are complete.

- Calls you, the borrower, to ask for more information when needed.

- Prepares all documents neatly for the underwriter to review.

Underwriter

- Works for the bank.

- Inspects the borrower's documents in close detail.

- Verifies that the information is accurate and follows bank guidelines.

- Stops the process if inconsistencies are found.

- Asks processor to ask borrower for more information.

- Gives the final stamp of approval when everything is okay.

Grant Team

- Works for city government or federal authorities (you will never meet with grant agents).

- Receives all your documents from the bank and reviews them to make sure they fulfill all necessary grant guidelines.

- Orders an environmental study to check for neighborhood problems such as infestation or extreme weather issues.

- Orders an inspection to check the property to see if it follows building codes. (This inspection is independent from your own inspection. You do not pay for it).

- Provides you a considerable amount of money to help pay closing costs and reduce the sales price of the home.

The Buyer's Real Estate Agent

- Works as a self-employed independent contractor or for a broker.

- Helps you find a home within your price range.

- Helps you submit an offer to a home seller.

- Helps negotiate a good deal for you.

- Helps you sign the contract.

- Recommends that you get an inspector.

- Helps negotiate with the seller's real estate agent about which repairs will be done.

- Keeps in touch with your loan officer to see how paperwork is moving along.

- Helps you find homeowner's insurance.

- Helps you solve little problems that rise during the process.

- Keeps in touch with everybody in the process.

The Seller's Real Estate Agent or Listing Agent

- Hired by a seller to sell his/her home.

- Assists the seller to help sell his/her home.

- Advertises the home in the multiple listing service.

- Places sign outside of home, and lockbox to allow easy access for realtors representing buyer.

- Provides the Seller's Disclosure Notice (the seller's opinion about the condition of the house).

- Holds open houses to show the home being sold.

- Negotiates contract on behalf of seller.

- Communicates with buyer's agent acting as the voice and direct representative of seller's interests.

The Title Processor

- Works for title company.

- Opens title upon receiving signed contract and earnest money from homebuyer.

- Places homebuyer's earnest money in an escrow account.

- Initiates a title search to make sure that the property you are buying does not have any liens against it.

- Provides a tax certification search to see how much you will be paying in property taxes.

- Provides you with title insurance to protect you and the lender from future title issues (such as an unexpected claim of ownership on the property).

- Prepares documents to be signed at the time of closing.

- Acts as an independent, neutral third party between buyer and seller.

The Inspector

- Works for himself/herself as an independent contractor.

- Hired by the homebuyer to do an inspection of the home.

- Does an onsite technical and mechanical inspection of the home you want to buy.

- Checks to see how all the systems of the home are working and whether they meet guidelines, including the electrical, heating and airconditioning, plumbing, foundation, and roof systems.

- Does a termite inspection. Some types of loans will require termite inspection as a mandatory requirement. You will be notified by lender if that is the case.

- Provides a report of items that seller can be asked to repair.

- Inspector is not a prophet and cannot know if something will break down later; the report is about the systems' current condition.

The Builder, contractor and workers

- Builder supervises the building of the home, making sure that it follows building codes.

- Contractor works for builder and hires workers to build the home.

- Workers build the home.

The Surveyor

- Works for self as an independent contractor.

- Measures the property lines of the lot.

- Checks whether there are utility or other easements, encroachments, etc., on the property.

- Provides a map or survey of the lot's perimeter.

- Annotates important information in the survey (such as whether the property is in a flood zone or not).

The Appraiser

- Works for self as an independent contractor.

- Does a comparative market analysis on the property.

- Writes up an appraisal report (an opinion of its value in the current market).

The Attorney

- Is responsible for overseeing that all legal documents are expedited properly (the Deed of Trust, General Warranty Deed with Vendor's Lien, Promissory Note, and so on). The title company hires the attorney here.

- You might want to hire your own attorney to advise you and protect your individual interests.

Homeowner's Insurance Agent

- Works for self as an independent contractor.

- Provides different quotes for homeowner's insurance depending on the coverage you want.

- Explains to you a breakdown of the coverage you will have.

- Explains important concepts (such as replacement cost, deductible, etc.).

- Gets you flood insurance if your house needs it.

The Escrow Agent

- Works for the title company.

- Is the last person in the home buying transaction.

- Is the neutral party (acts as middleman between buyer and seller) that has you sign all the paperwork at closing.

- Facilitates the signing of the documents at closing, including explanation of the main points contained in the Deed of Trust, the Promissory Note, The General Warranty Deed with Vendor's Lien and others.

Check List of Standard Documents Used During the Homebuying Process

Lender Documents

- ☐ 1003 or Loan Application
- ☐ Good Faith Estimate
- ☐ Truth in Lending Disclosure Statement
- ☐ Private Disclosure Form
- ☐ Borrower Certification and Authorization
- ☐ Borrower Signature Authorization
- ☐ Disclosure Notice
- ☐ Equal Credit Opportunity Act
- ☐ The Housing Financial Discrimination Act of 1977 Fair Lending Notice
- ☐ Privacy Disclosure Notice
- ☐ Notice of Applicant Right to Receive Copy of Appraisal Report
- ☐ Texas Mortgage Broker/Loan Officer Disclosure
- ☐ Servicing Disclosure Statement
- ☐ Mortgage Loan Origination Agreement

- ☐ Consent Credit Verfification Employment
- ☐ Form 4506 T
- ☐ Property Insurance Requirement
- ☐ Affiliated Business Disclosure

Documents for FHA Loans or Federal Home Administration Loans

- ☐ HUD-Addendum to Uniform Residential Loan
- ☐ For Your Protection, Get a Home Inspection
- ☐ Important Notice to Homebuyer
- ☐ FHA: Energy Efficient Mortgage

Grant Documents

- ☐ Homeownership Education Certificate
- ☐ Signed FHA Loan Underwriting and Transmittal Summary (HUD 92900-LT 5/2008)
- ☐ Good Faith Estimate from Lender (include signed disclosures)
- ☐ Form 1003 (Uniform Residential Loan Application)
- ☐ Copy of Credit Report for all Applicants
- ☐ Verification of Employment for all adult members and the last three months of paycheck stubs
- ☐ The last six months of bank statements

- ☐ Verification of Rent
- ☐ Copy of Fully Executed Contract of Sale (must be legible with no cross-outs)
- ☐ Exhibit A Information (DAP only)
- ☐ Clearance for EPLS and OFAC on Lender's Letterhead
- ☐ Downpayment Assistance Loan Application
- ☐ Property Data Sheet info
- ☐ Terms and Conditions
- ☐ Conflict of Interests
- ☐ Form 1010
- ☐ Affidavits of Residency (notarized and original signatures)
- ☐ Affidavit of Homeownership
- ☐ Harris County Community Services Department/Down-payment Assistance Program and Neighborhood Stabilization Program Registration Form (ORIGINAL)
- ☐ Affidavit of Selling Parties (Original signatures)
- ☐ Notice to Real Property Owner/Seller (Original signature)
- ☐ Total Family Income Worksheet
- ☐ Single Family Home Inspection Request Form
- ☐ Exhibit A

- ☐ Home Eligibility Release Form
- ☐ Recapture Disclosure
- ☐ Notification Watch Out for Lead-Based Paint Poisoning
- ☐ Notice Concerning Inspections
- ☐ Borrower's Signature Authorization
- ☐ Entitlement of Funds
- ☐ Certification of Zero Income
- ☐ Verification of Assets Disposed
- ☐ Applicant(s) Certification
- ☐ Applicant(s) Certification Continued
- ☐ Affidavit of Applicant(s) Income
- ☐ Funds Disclosure
- ☐ Flood Determination Form

Real Estate Agent Documents

- ☐ Residential Buyer/Tenant Representation Agreement
- ☐ Information about Brokerage Services
- ☐ Broker Notice to Buyer/Tenant
- ☐ One to Four Family Residential Contract
- ☐ Third Party Financing Addendum for Credit Approval
- ☐ Seller's Disclosure Notice

- ☐ Addendum for Seller's Disclosure of Information on Lead-Based Paint and Lead-Based Paint Hazards as Required by Federal Law
- ☐ Information About Special Flood Hazard Areas
- ☐ Addendum for Property Subject to Mandatory Membership in a Property Owner Association
- ☐ Notice to a Purchaser of Real Property in a Water District

Homeowner's Insurance Documents

- ☐ Insurance Binder

Title Commitment Documents

- ☐ Commitment for Title

  Schedule A
  Schedule B (Exceptions from Coverage)
  Schedule C
  Schedule D
  Privacy Policy Notice
  Tax Certificate
  HOA Certificate

Closing Documents

- ☐ HUD-1
- ☐ Promissory Note
- ☐ Federal Truth in Lending Disclosure Statement
- ☐ Deed of Trust
- ☐ Mineral Rights Acknowledegment and Agreement
- ☐ Important Information about Your Privacy
- ☐ Servicing Disclosure Statement
- ☐ No Oral Agreements
- ☐ Privacy Policy Notice
- ☐ Borrower's Certification and Authorization Certification
- ☐ Rights of Parties in Possession Affidavits
- ☐ Authorization to Release Information
- ☐ Request for Taxpayer Identification Number and Certification
- ☐ Statement of Occupancy
- ☐ Collateral Protection Insurance Disclosure
- ☐ First Payment Notice
- ☐ Rights of Parties in Possession Affidavits
- ☐ Notice to Purchasers regarding Property Taxes
- ☐ Survey

☐ Survey Disclosure

☐ Tax Proration Agreement

☐ Errors and Omissions Agreement

☐ Title Insurance

☐ The Title Abstract

☐ Escrow Analysis

Median Income Guideline Chart for 2013 in Houston, Texas (Helps you understand if you are eligible for grants)

This chart is intended for homebuyers who want to know if they qualify for housing grants.

To confirm accuracy of the figures listed below, please verify with the appropriate grant providers. Please note that income guidelines are usually adjusted yearly.

To have a better understanding of whether you truly qualify for grants or not, I recommend that you ask a loan officer who is knowledgeable about grants and who knows how they work.

This calculation can get pretty complex.

Family Size	80% "median household" income	110% "median household" income	115% "median household" income	120% "median household" income
1 person	$37,100	$51,040	$53,350	$55,650
2 people	$42,400	$58,300	$60,950	$63,600
3 people	$47,700	$65,560	$68,550	$71,550
4 people	$52,950	$72,820	$76,150	$79,450
5 people	$57,200	$78,650	$82,250	$85,850
6 people	$61,450	$84,480	$88,350	$92,200
7 people	$65,700	$90,310	$94,450	$98,550
8 people	$69,900	$96,140	$100,550	$104,900

Useful Websites for Homebuyers

Credit

www.annualcreditreport.com
www.creditcoalition.org
www.wesleyhousehouston.org

Budget, Income, Expenses, and Savings

www.covenantcapital.org

Grants

For homes within the city of Houston, see:
http://www.houstontx.gov/houstonhope

For homes in Pasadena, Fort Bend, Waller, Matagorda etc., see: http://www.sethfc.com/current_programs.htm

For homes outside of the city of Houston and within Harris County, www.hrc.hctx.net/dap.htm

For homebuyers with disabilities who want to buy a home in Harris county (outside of the city limits of Houston),

Montgomery, or Ft. Bend Counties, see:

http://texashoyo.accesstexashousing.org/ houston.htm

For foreclosed homes outside of the city of Houston and within Harris County through the Neighborhood Stabilization Program, see:

www.csd.hctx.net/ps neighborhoodstabiliza- tionprogram.aspx

To see if you can qualify for savings matching accounts grants offered by Covenant Community Capital Corporation, see: www.covenantcapital.org

To see if you qualify for Bond 77:

http://www.tdhca.state.tx.us/homeowner-ship/fthb/down-payment-assistance.htm

To see if you qualify for a mortgage credit certificate or *MCC* see: www.tdhca.state.tx.us/homeownership/ fthb/mort credertificate.htm

Home-buying class

For a list of HUD housing approved agencies, see:

http://www.houstontx.gov/housing/home- buyer.html

Homestead exemption

If you want to download homestead exemption forms and check property values at the Harris County Appraisal District website go to: www.hcad.org

Interest rates

Search interest rates at: www.bankrate.com

Home Search

Search for resale homes in the Houston area at: www.har.com

Search for homes sold directly from seller to buyer at: www.forsalebyowner.com

Homeowner's insurance

If you want to check whether the property you are buying is in a flood zone, see: www.tsarp.org

Protesting Property Taxes in Houston

If you want to protest your taxes in Houston go to: www.hcad.org

Glossary

Actual Cash Value: One of the viable options offered by homeowner insurance companies when selecting an insurance plan that protects your home in case of loss. Since it offers the cost of replacing the property minus depreciation, this option is not as preferable an option as replacement cost that offers better coverage.

Adjustable Rate Mortgages: Loans that adjust (increase or decrease) depending on the conditions of the market. ARMS change at the same rate as a national interest rate index that reflects current financial conditions like the Treasury bill rate. ARMS have caps on the amount the interest can change. The interest can never go higher or lower than the caps. ARMS have two components: 1. the *market index* selected by the bank and the 2. *margin* (the charge the lender adds to the index and passes on to the the consumer).

Amortized loan A bank loan is repaid in a series of installments, a portion of which is applied to reduce the principal amount of the loan and a portion that is applied to pay interest. At the beginning of the loan, the repayment formula allocates a larger portion to interest payment than to principal reduction.

Annual percentage rate (APR): An APR is a calculation for the consumer's protection that can be used to compare the closing costs different lenders will charge you. The APR is always higher than the interest rate provided to the client by the loan officer, because it includes some closing costs and some prepaid items. Please note this is not the same APR calculation used with your credit card.

Appraisal: Estimate or opinion of property value. Values are determined by one of three methods: 1. Sales comparison approach where the house you are buying is compared to similar homes located around the neighborhood that have been recently sold. This is the most frequently used method for residential properties 2. The cost approach determines the value of a home by calculating how much if would cost to replace the home after subtracting accrued depreciation, and 3. The income approach where the value of the property is determined by estimating how much income and return on investment the property can generate. It is used on commercial properties such as rental apartments, strip malls etc.

Appraiser: Professional hired by the lender to estimate the value of the property you want to buy.

Arbitration: One of the procedures that can be selected to settle differences between buyer and seller through the court system. In arbitration, the arbitrator hears evidence and receives testimony, much like a judge, and makes a binding decision. The other procedure most commonly used is mediation.

Bankruptcy: A voluntary legal procedure that consumers are allowed to do when unable to repay outstanding debt. Bankruptcy offers an opportunity to start fresh by forgiving debts that cannot be paid while offering creditors a chance to obtain some measure of repayment based on what assets are available. There are three options when filing bankruptcy: 1. Chapter 7 –involves liquidation of assets, 2. Chapter 13-debt repayment plan adapted to consumer's possibilities 3. Chapter 11-re-organization of individual or company's assets.

Binding: Describes a strong mutual agreement that a buyer and seller commit to when they execute (both sign) a contract. If it is broken, there can be legal consequences.

Bond 77: An excellent way for first-time buyers who are higher earners to get down payment assistance to pay for their closing costs. These programs are available at select mortgage banks as determined by TDHCA (Texas Department of Housing and Community Affairs).

Budget: An estimate of income, expenses and savings for a set period of time.

Buyer's market: A market that has more sellers than buyers. Lower prices result from this excess of supply over demand.

Buyer Tenant Representation Agreement: A contract signed at the beginning of the home buying process between real estate agent and buyer.

Buyer's real estate agent: A real estate agent who only represents the buyer.

Capacity to pay: The ability to repay a mortgage because one has income or assets.

Capital: The amount of money a consumer has to make a down payment, pay for closing costs, and keep in reserve to buy a home. Lender's history shows that the more the borrower contributes of his own money to pay for expenses, the more likely he is to repay the loan he owes to the bank.

Cash value: One of the options homebuyers have when choosing hazard insurance. It refers to being provided the cash value only of a home if physically destroyed.

Closing costs and prepaids: Costs paid in addition to the down payment on closing day.

Collateral: Property pledged as security to a debt. The house you are buying will be collateral or security for the loan. You give the lender your promise to repay the mortgage and the right to take the house and sell it if you cannot, or do not pay back the loan.

Collections: Money that the consumer owes to third-party vendors as a result of not paying an original debt. It includes added fees and interest.

Comparative Market Analysis: A CMA is a method of finding out how much the home is worth in the market by comparing it to current and recent home values in the same neighborhood.

Conventional Loans: Provided by private lending institutions that follow particular guidelines. Lenders set their own interest rates and fees, and determine the maximum amount they will lend under each program. Typical qualifying ratios are 28/36. Customarily they require higher credit scores, lower debt to income ratios, mortgage insurance and amount of fees vary depending on credit scores and compensating factors.

Contract: An agreement between buyer and seller with the intention of creating a legal obligation.

Closing: The last step that completes the home buying transaction when buyers (and sellers) sign papers.

Conditional preapproval. A lender's commitment to provide a loan to a homebuyer, provided that all conditions are met.

Credit bureau: An agency that researches and collects individual credit information and sells it to creditors so they can make decisions about granting loans.

Credit card: A card issued by a financial company giving the holder an option to borrow funds.

Credit limit: The maximum amount of credit that a financial institution extends to a client.

Creditor: A person or institution to whom money is owed.

Credit report: A detailed report of an individual's credit history, prepared by a credit bureau and used by a lender to determine a loan applicant's creditworthiness.

Credit score: A numerical expression based on a statistical analysis of a person's credit files that represent his or her creditworthiness.

Debt-to-income ratio: A figure that calculates how much of a person's income is spent paying debts. The more monthly income one devotes to paying back debts, the higher one's debt-to-income ratio. Usually, a homebuyer's monthly debt payments cannot be more than 25 to 28 percent of gross monthly income and all the buyer's monthly debt cannot total more than 33 to 36 percent of monthly income.

Deductible: In an insurance policy, a deductible is the amount that an insured must pay out of pocket toward a claim before the insurer will pay anything toward it.

Deed of Trust: A legal document where a homebuyer deeds the property he is buying to a trust that holds it for the benefit of a lender. In other words, the property is pledged as collateral or security for a loan until the home-buyer has repaid the loan.

Deed restrictions: Regulations that apply to a group of homes or lots in a specific development.

Disputes: Regarding credit reports, disputes are arguments or claims against mistakes that affect a homebuyer's creditworthiness.

Earnest money: A small amount of money that a seller requires a potential buyer to deposit in an escrow account before a home buying transaction is completed. The purpose of earnest money is to show the seller the buyer's commitment and intention of buying the seller's property. If the transaction closes, earnest money is applied towards closing costs or down payment. If it does not, it can be returned or not to the homebuyer depending on the terms established in the contract.

Easements: On a survey, easements are a legal right to cross or otherwise use someone else's land for a specified purpose.

Elevation survey: In some geographical areas known for having unstable soil, some homebuyers prefer to order a special kind of survey called elevation survey. These offer measurements that show degrees of movement of the home within a certain time period. Homebuyers can learn "how level/out of level" the foundation of a home has become over the years. The elevation points of this kind of survey are critical points of your home's foundation that are un-level in relation to the ground itself where your foundation lies. It is frequently used as a benchmark to monitor future structural movements of the home in relation to the ground it lies on.

Encroachment: A structure or other item belonging to one property that crosses a boundary line into another.

Energy efficiency: Saving energy with energy-efficient features and equipment.

Environmental report: Report generated by a qualified firm to determine potential environmental hazards. The report will indicate the likelihood of contamination or pollution.

Equifax: A consumer credit-reporting agency that provides credit ratings to lenders and consumers.

Equity: The difference between the current market value of a property and the amount the owner still owes on the mortgage.

Escrow: A trust account held in the borrower's name to pay obligations such as property taxes and insurance premiums.

Escrow account: A separate account where funds are safeguarded until a transaction has been completed. In real estate transactions, earnest money is usually held in escrow with a title company.

Escrow agent: A neutral, third party title company agent who acts as a go-between for buyer and seller during the home buying process. The agent's job is to ensure that all conditions of a real estate transaction are properly met. The escrow agent keeps the original purchase contract, and earnest money safely, and makes sure all the people involved in the home-buying process are doing their jobs.

Establishing good credit: The act of building up good credit history by using credit responsibly (such as credit cards).

Expenses: An outflow of money to another person or group to pay for an item or service.

Experian: One of the largest credit bureaus in the United States. Gathers information about consumers and provides credit ratings to lenders and consumers.

Fair Credit Reporting Act: It was created to ensure accuracy and privacy of the information contained in consumer credit reports by credit reporting agencies. The act entitles the consumer to dispute inaccuracies in the credit report and have them removed if they are not verified by the credit agencies.

Fannie Mae: The Federal National Mortgage Association, a government-sponsored enterprise whose purpose is to expand the secondary mortgage market by securitizing mortgages. This allows lenders to reinvest their assets into more loans.

Federal Truth in Lending: A legal document that discloses meaningful information about the cost of the money a consumer borrows. It is provided upon applying for a loan.

FHA loan: FHA stands for Federal Housing Administration. FHA loans are insured by the federal government, guaranteeing payment of the debt in case of default by the owner. They are typically designed to assist borrowers who are unable to get approved for conventional home loans. An FHA down-payment is usually three percent of the purchase price. You are required to pay a monthly insurance premium until the outstanding principal balance of your loan reaches 78%; there are limits on the amount of money you can borrow. Debt to income ratios are 29/41.

Fixed interest rate: A loan or mortgage with an interest rate that will remain at a predetermined rate for its entire term.

First-time homebuyer: Someone who has had no present ownership interest in a principal residence during the two-year period ending on the date of acquisition of the principal residence. (In the case of married persons, if one spouse does not qualify as a first-time buyer, both spouses are disqualified.)

Fixed installment loans: A loan that is repaid in fixed, regular installments and has a rate of interest fixed for the duration of the loan.

Flood zone: A geographical area shown on a Flood Hazard Boundary Map or a Flood Insurance Rate Map that reflects the severity or type of flooding in the area.

For-sale-by-owner: Also known as a FSBO. A home sold without the representation of a real estate broker or agent.

Foreclosure: A specific legal process in which a lender attempts to recover the balance of a loan from a borrower who has stopped making payments by forcing the sale of the assets as the collateral for the home.

Foreclosed home: A foreclosed home has been repossessed by the lender after the owner stopped making mortgage loan payments.

Freddie Mac: The Federal Home Loan Mortgage Corporation, a government-sponsored enterprise created to expand the secondary market for homeowners. It allows an increased supply of money available for mortgage lending and increases the money available for new home purchases.

Good Faith Estimate: A legal document provided to the homebuyer shortly after the loan application is approved.

It contains an estimate of all the expenses of buying the home. The Good Faith Estimate, shown at the beginning of the process, and the HUD-1at the end of the process should be very similar.

Grants: Free money provided to some first-time home-buyers that will not have to be paid back as long as guide-lines are followed.

HAR: The Houston Association of Realtors, an organization that supports real estate agents and consumers with the buying and selling of homes. HAR offers a website: www.har.com where consumers can search for all listed homes in Houston.

Hard hit: A kind of credit pull by creditors that can affect your credit adversely (it can lower your credit score by about five points for six months). If you get a store credit card just to save 10 percent on a single purchase, you have hurt your credit score. A good rule of thumb is to try to avoid any inquiries that are considered hard pulls.

Homestead exemption: A legal regulation to protect the value of the residential homeowners from creditors and other circumstances arising from the death of a home-owner's spouse. One of the advantages of filing for home-stead exemption when you buy a home for use as your primary residence is that you are given an average of 18-20 percent discount (give or take) off the value of your property taxes. For instance, if your annual property taxes were to be $3,000 a year. You could get a discount of $600 and pay $2400. Homestead exemption in Texas needs to be filed only once.

HOA: Homeowners' Association is an organization created by a real estate developer for the purpose of controlling the appearance of a residential subdivision and managing any common-area assets.

Homeowner's insurance: Commonly called hazard insurance, it is property insurance that covers private homes in case of fire, storms, theft, liability against third parties, and so on. It is required if you are getting a mortgage.

Homeowner's warranty policy: Insurance to protect your home after you have closed on your home. It protects you against the cost of repair bills if the heating, plumbing, air conditioning, or appliances break down during the first year you own your home. If the home is brand new, most builders provide their own warranty that covers at least the standard residential building requirements demanded from builders. If the home is a resale home, a one-year warranty residential warranty can be purchased by buyer or seller. Coverage varies depending on type of warranty purchased. A home warranty policy usually charges you an annual premium and a flat fee per service call. Homebuyer is recommended to do their own due diligence to inquire about different policies and coverages.

House poor: When a homeowner 's house payments are too high in proportion to income.

HUD: The United States Department of Housing and Urban Development, also known as HUD is a cabinet department in the executive branch of the United States Federal Government established in 1965 during the Presidency of Lyndon Johnson. Its purpose was to develop and execute policies on housing and to protect the consumer against abuses caused in the real estate transaction. Professionals who do real estate need to abide by these regulations. Presently it oversees and administers federal programs dealing with better housing and urban renewal.

HUD-1 or Settlement Statement: A document prepared by a closing or escrow agent at the time of closing describing the breakdown of the closing costs that is signed at the closing table. By law, the numbers listed in the HUD or Settlement Statement, should not vary more than a certain percentage from the numbers quoted to you by the loan officer in the Good Faith Estimate.

HUD homes: Foreclosed houses owned by Housing and Urban Development that were once financed with FHA loans and now are sold at a discount.

HVAC: Heating, ventilation and air conditioning. Refers to the integrated heating and cooling systems installed in most residential properties in the United States.

Income: The amount of money received during a period of time in exchange for labor or services.

IDA: Independent Development Accounts or Matching Savings Program. It allows many lower-income families to save, build assets, and enter the financial mainstream with a grant that doubles or triples the amount saved toward a down payment on a home-purchase.

Information about Brokerage Services: A document that is signed by a homebuyer and real estate agent at the beginning of the transaction that establishes the agent's responsibilities to the buyer.

Inspector: Qualified professional who is hired to check the structure and the mechanical parts of a property and evaluates if it meets construction and code guidelines. The inspector is in charge of writing a report describing the condition of the home in its current state. Inspectors can also provide good advice on normal maintenance practices

such as changing the filters of the home and cleaning off the gutters, once you have bought the home.

Interest: The charge homeowners pay to the bank for borrowing money.

Intermediary: In real estate, it refers to a real estate agent who represents the buyer and seller of the same home at the same time.

Installment loan: A credit account in which the amount of the payment and the number of payments are predetermined or fixed.

Interest rate: The percentage of interest lenders charge to buyers.

IRS: The Internal Revenue Service, the Department of the Treasury that taxes Americans with income in the United States.

Judgment: A court decree stating that one individual or entity owes money to another.

Listing real estate agent: Professional in the real estate transaction hired by the seller to sell a property.

Loan officer: Professional hired by a bank or mortgage company to do residential loans.

Median Household Income: Defined by the U.S. Census Bureau as the amount which divides the income distribution into two equal groups, half having income about that amount, and half having income below that amount. Down-payment assistant programs use median household income as their base to determine homebuyer's eligibility for grants.

Mediation: A nonbinding process where a neutral party works with buyer and seller to reach a mutually agreeable settlement. If a settlement is not reached, the mediator has no authority to impose one on the parties.

More than the minimum due: When paying back your credit card debt, it is advisable to pay more than the minimum required by the creditor. Doing this can make a significant impact on your monthly budget and increase your credit score.

MCC: Mortgage Credit Certificate. Issued by certain state or local governments to allow a taxpayer to claim a tax credit for some portion of the mortgage interest paid during a given tax year.

Mortgage: A loan secured by real property. When you buy a house, you give the lender a note and mortgage on your house. The mortgage secures your house as collateral or security for the loan in case you stop your payments.

The lender has the right to sell your house and pay off the loan.

Mortgage Insurance Premium: When applying for an FHA loan, MIP is a fee that is paid by the homebuyer to protect the lender in case of default. There are two types of fees involved in an FHA loan: 1. An upfront mortgage insurance premium fee that is paid at the time of closing, and 2. A monthly charge as part of your mortgage payment. MIP is supposed to be automatically cancelled when the mortgage balance reaches 78% of the original value of the house.

Notice to Buyer Tenant: A legal document that the homebuyer signs to acknowledge that a real estate agent has advised the buyer to do a residential inspection and environmental report.

MUD taxes: Municipal Utilities Taxes. An extra tax that homebuyers pay if they buy a property in a MUD District. It covers the cost of providing public utilities such as water, electricity, natural gas, sewage treatment, waste collection and management, wholesale telecommunications to the residents of that district.

Multiple Listing Service: A service provided to consumers and real estate agents where listed homes are advertised.

Offer: A written purchase proposal signed by a homebuyer showing intent to buy the seller's property. The offer includes earnest money as a good faith deposit. An offer only has the initials and signature of the buyer and doesn't become a binding contract until seller has also signed it.

Option period: A specified period of time when the buyer can choose to either continue with purchase or terminate the contract before the period expires. An option fee, if paid, acts as a guarantee that the seller will not accept an offer from someone else until the potential buyer has made a decision within the option period. Option periods give homebuyers the right to retract from the contract, and allow them to receive their earnest money back.

Option fee: A payment a buyer makes to a seller to buy the option of withdrawing from the contract within an option period.

Post-tension cables: Preferred method of building foundations used by many builders in unstable soil areas of the country. The method consists of adding cables to the foundation that allows movement of the home without sacrificing structural integrity of the property.

Preapproval letter: A letter from a lender informing a buyer how much money can be borrowed.

Pre-closing costs: Expenses a buyer pays out of pocket before the home closes.

Prequalification letter: A letter from a mortgage lender that states a buyer is prequalified to buy a home but does not commit the lender to a particular mortgage amount. These letters are often considered being not worth the paper they are printed on. They are much less substantial than preapproval letters.

Principal and Interest: Principal is the amount borrowed from the lender, while interest is the charge paid to the lender to borrow the money.

Private Mortgage Insurance: On conventional financing, PMI is an added expense to the buyer that protects the lender in case of default. It is required with loans where the buyer puts down less than a 20 percent down payment.

Promissory note: A document signed at closing by the homebuyer containing a written promise to repay the lender a stated sum according to agreed terms. The note includes monthly payment amounts, payment due dates, details about how to submit payments, and information about penalty fees for late payments, and what can happen if you violate the terms of this note.

Property line: The boundary line between two pieces of property

Property taxes: A tax the homeowner is obligated to pay to municipalities. It is based on the estimated value of the property.

Quitclaim deed: An efficient quick legal procedure to transfer interest in a property from the owner of the property (called the grantor) to the recipient of the property (called the grantee). Unlike most other property deeds, a quitclaim deed contains no warranty that protects the recipient for claims that might arise in the future. It only covers whatever interest the grantor actually possesses at the time of the transfer. Quitclaim deeds are rarely used to transfer property from seller to buyer in a traditional property sale. Because of this lack of warranty, quitclaim deeds are most often used to transfer property between family members, or in divorce, whereby the spouse terminates any interest in the jointly owned property, thereby granting the spouse full rights to the property. It can also be used while auctioning a property, and local other government official's claim having no interest in the property, but only that, which allows them to recover unpaid taxes.

226

www.homesatyourfingertips.com

Real estate agent: A professional who can help you buy or sell your home.

Real estate broker: An individual licensed to negotiate and arrange real estate transactions, who by virtue of amount of time spent, representing buyers and sellers, and advanced education acquired, has achieved the highest license available. The broker is authorized to hire real estate agents to work under the broker's supervision.

Replacement cost. The amount it would cost an insurance company to rebuild a home in case of total loss or damage. This option is different from the actual cash value option and preferred since it has more coverage.

Repossession of a car: The right a creditor may have to repossess a car if car loan payments are late. In many states, creditors or lessors can do this legally without going to court or warning a consumer in advance.

Resale homes: Homes that have already been lived in. Many of them are posted in the Multiple Listing Service (in Houston, the website is www.har.com).

Revolving credit. A credit account where the available credit continually fluctuates up and down. When credit is used, available credit decreases. When the loan is repaid, available credit increases (up to the maximum available).

Those that issue revolving lines of credit do so with the intention of making a profit.

Sellers Disclosure Notice: Standard *Texas Real Estate Commission* document that seller needs to complete upon selling his property. It is supposed to show true conditions of the home he is selling.

Setback line: Also called building line is the distance from the street or edge of your lot that you cannot build in. A setback line can be in the front, side and back yard. You can find building lines by looking at your property survey or the title policy you received when you purchased your home.

Short sale properties: Homes of which owners owe more money than home is worth in the market. Often used as an alternative to foreclosure because it lessens costs to both the creditor and borrower; however, either course of action often results in a negative credit consequence for the property owner.

Soft hit: Also known as a soft inquiry, it is a type of inquiry into a credit history that does not adversely affect the credit score.

Sold as is: Properties where the seller is not willing to do any repairs. Many foreclosed homes are sold as is.

Survey: A document that shows the boundary lines of a home, encroachments, easements, elevations, and other important features related to the land of a property.

Surveyor: A person who surveys a property to determine boundary lines, encroachments, easements, flood zones, and so on.

Tax certificate: An investigation issued by a tax service showing the current year's taxes, the last year the taxes were paid, and any delinquencies to be collected before or at closing.

TREC: Texas Real Estate Commission. The agency that oversees real estate activity in Texas.

Title Company: Company that does the title search, issues the title policy, and performs the closing of a home buying process.

Title insurance: Protects the homebuyer and lender against financial loss from defects in title to real property and from the invalidity or unenforceability of mortgage liens. A title insurance policy promises to pay for a loss as a result of claims arising out of title or ownership problems that could have been discovered in the public records, and also those called no-record defects that could not be discovered in the records even with the most complete search (such as forgery, impersonation, capacity of parties, faulty acknowledgements and mechanic and material liens). A title policy will not only protect the insured for as long as they have an interest in the property, but it will also protect their heirs and devisees for as long as they hold title to the property.

Title insurance companies: In real estate transactions, title companies are in charge of executing title searches, issuing title policies, and acting as go-in-betweens buyers and sellers throughout real estate transactions.

Title policy: A document that shows the buyer has clear ownership of a property. A loan does not usually close until the title company has assured the lender that there are no hidden problems with a title to a piece of property.

TransUnion: One of the "Big Three" credit-reporting bureaus in the United States that gather financial information about consumers.

Truth in Lending: Document provided by the lender to the consumer disclosing the annual percentage rate of the loan, including interest and other fees charged. It contains a summary of the total cost of credit, expressed as a yearly rate or APR. The APR includes the interest rate, points, and certain fees that you are required to pay. It also provides other data about the loan like finance charges, the schedule

of payment, the total amount of all payments, late payment charges and whether there is a pre-payment charge.

Truth in Lending Act: A federal law obligating a lender to give full written disclosure of all fees, terms, and conditions associated with the loan.

Underwriter: The professional hired by the bank in charge of reviewing the homebuyers' capacity to repay the loan, the cash or capital available, the credit risk to the bank, and the condition of the home you are buying as collateral to secure the loan. The underwriter compares your information with the lending policies of the bank and determines whether or not to recommend the loan. The loan committee makes the final loan decision, but the underwriter's opinion is of critical importance.

VA loan: VA stands for Veterans Administration, which provides home loans to veterans or veterans' relatives. These loans are fully guaranteed by the federal government in case of a homebuyer's default.

Voluntary repossession of a car: A term used to describe a situation in which a consumer voluntarily surrenders a car after falling behind on loan payments. It does not liberate a consumer from paying the outstanding debt.

Variable interest rate: Amount of compensation to a lender that is allowed to vary over the maturity of a loan, typically governed by an appropriate index.

Warranty deed with vendors' lien: A type of deed where the seller guarantees that he or she holds clear title to a piece of real estate and can transfer ownership or title to the buyer. It conveys real property to buyer with a warranty of title, and a warranty of no encumbrances, but, reserves an outstanding lien that needs to be paid to the lender. The lien exists until the full purchase price is paid off, so the seller or the vendor has the right to sell the property back if he/she is not paid in full.

Warranty deed: A legal instrument or document used to transfer ownership of real estate. It is unique to real property, because real property is more likely to have limitations, conditions, and claims against its ownership.

Credits

Can Stock Photo and Morgue File have facilitated the clip art included herein:

1   Home held in hand (cover), (c) csp 6625777. Uploaded by: Nexus Plexus

2   Man going crazy, (c) csp 5762457. Uploaded by: camicubus

3   Toolbox, (c) csp 9131864. Uploaded by: RaStudio

4   *Who, Where, Why, What, When,* (c) csp 7418437. Uploaded by: PixelsAway

5   *What, If,* (c) csp 7495339. Uploaded by: PixelsAway

6   *Go,* (c) csp 7334886. Uploaded by: d3images

7   *Actnow,* (c) csp 3655365. Uploaded by: iqoncept

8   *Yes,* (c) csp 2146049. Uploaded by: pdesign

9   *Hurry,* (c) csp 8722696. Uploaded by iqoncept

10 Man supporting house, (c) csp 4948714. Uploaded by: erierika

11 Homebuyer instructor, (c) csp 5423065. Uploaded by: artenot

12 *Ask questions,* (c) csp 1869792. Uploaded by: iquoncept

13 *Grow,* (c) csp 1869923. Uploaded by: iquoncept

14 *Learn,* (c) csp 6565257. Uploaded by: fantasista

15 Homebuyer counselor, (c) csp 6717362. Uploaded by: lenm

16 *Bad Credit/Good Credit,* (c) csp 5455022. Uploaded by: iquoncept

17 Exclamation mark, (c) csp 3948757. Uploaded by: GeorgiosArt

18 Pizza, morguefile, image url: htpp://mrg. bz/AhvT50

19 Man doing budget, (c) csp 6111256. Uploaded by: davisales

20 Dollar with belt, (c) csp 1855998. Uploaded by: cienpies

21 Cutting debt, (c) csp 6839581. Uploaded by: alexmillos

22 Rocking chair: morguefile, image url:http//mrg.bz/Hn6Nel

23 *Can You Afford It?,* (c) csp 8994513. Uploaded by: iquoncept

24 Slow down, (c) csp 2374795. Uploaded by: iquoncept

25 Calculator problem solution, (c) csp 7259517. Uploaded by iquoncept

26 Woman/man conversation, (c) csp 2697268. Uploaded by: michaeldb

27 Lightbulb, (c) csp 5259277. Uploaded by: yayayoyo

28 Magnifying glass, morguefile, image http://mrg.bz/bNPdGg

29 Loan officer bubble, (c) csp 8959927. Uploaded by: Yury

30 Happy loan officer, (c) csp 8987821. Uploaded by: Yury

31 Green thumbs up, (c) csp 2146164. Uploaded by: pdesign

32 Coins out of bucket, morguefile, by Cohdra, Image: http://mrg.bz/4r7W6A

33 Real estate agent, (c) csp 4680964. Uploaded by: 9 lives

34 Victorian house, morguefile, By: kirk- 10kirk, image http://mrg.bz/9ZHB2B

35 *Make an offer*, (c) csp 2262421. Uploaded by iquoncept

36 Real estate contract, (c) csp 8040623. Uploaded by: cteconsulting

37 Contract with magnifying glass, (c) csp 1078428. Uploaded by: robynmac

38 Checkbooks, morguefile, http://mrg.bz/ n53vOf

39 Inspector examining house, (c) csp 3669653. Uploaded by: RTimages

40 Title reading, (c) csp 8987340. Uploaded by: Yury

41 Reading book, (c) csp 3538577. Uploaded by: MarketOlya

42 Homes/appraisal, (c) csp 4628441. Uploaded by: ctconsulting

43 *Evaluation/Outstanding*, (c) csp 2895345. Uploaded by michaeldb

44 Surveyor, (c) csp 5926483. Uploaded by: jamesschipper

45 Insurance agent, (c) csp 4673673. Uploaded by:hjalmeida

46 Flooded house, (c) csp 7790750. Uploaded by: cteconsulting

47 Closing, (c) csp 4670672. Uploaded by: davisales

48 Smily face, (c) csp 2225222. Uploaded by: Vladyslav

49 Real estate agent red dress, (c) csp 1005591. Uploaded by: Nikonas

50 Give me five, (c) csp 1855068. Uploaded by: pdesign

51 Handshake, (c) csp 6942860. Uploaded by: violetas

52 Animals of the jungle, (c) csp 3550455. Uploaded by: dagadu

53 Loan officer, (c) csp 7039096. Uploaded by: davisales

54 Loan processor, (c) csp 8976333. Uploaded by: Yury

55 Underwriter, (c) csp 5153300. Uploaded by: HitToon

56 Grant team call center, (c) csp 5286085. Uploaded by: moneca

57 Listing agent, (c) csp 2727264. Uploaded by: lenm

58 Title processor, (c) csp 3088203. Uploaded by: marish

59 Builder, (c) csp 8905157. Uploaded by: keltt

60 Appraiser, (c) csp 8777862. Uploaded by: photography33

61 Homes comparative, (c) csp 0306634. Uploaded by: prawny

62 Lawyer, (c) csp 8958031. Uploaded by: Yury

63 Escrow agent hurray, (c) csp 4451672. Uploaded by: wacker

64 Title insurance, (c) csp 5771269. Uploaded by: stevanovicigor

65 Derek Herrold, Networldintercative.com, provided credit pie image

66 Rosa Magaña, Farmers Insurance: Consultation in matters of homeowner's insurance